D1602489

TENACIOUS

TENACIOUS

BE A
Champion
of
CHANGE

Behind the Scenes Perspective from the Coach's Wife
Penni Leigh Graham

Foreword by
Todd Graham

Clovercroft Publishing

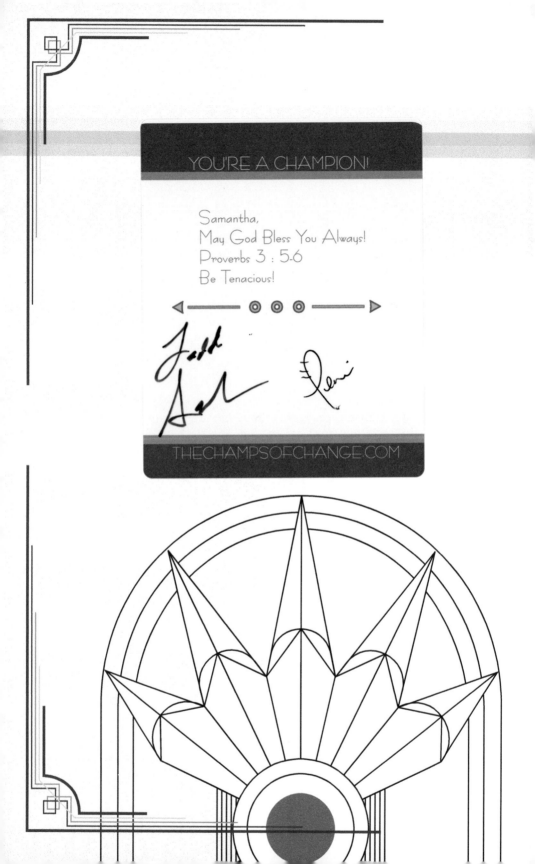

YOU'RE A CHAMPION!

Samantha,
May God Bless You Always!
Proverbs 3 : 5-6
Be Tenacious!

THECHAMPSOFCHANGE.COM

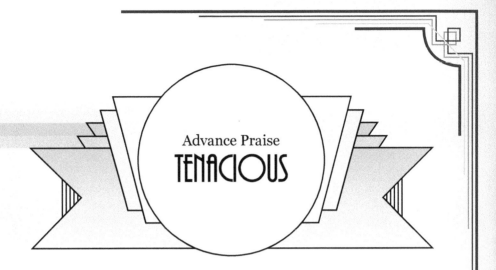

Advance Praise

TENACIOUS

"Tenacious is part motivational, part strategic thinking, part overcoming adversity, and 100 percent about winning. This book gives people the tools to persevere and accomplish great goals. It teaches what Todd and Penni refer to as 'The Graham Game Plan,' which embraces hard work over entitlement, and preaches commitment over compromise."

Dr. Jack Graham is the pastor of Prestonwood Baptist Church, one of the nation's largest and most dynamic congregations. Jack is a noted author of numerous books. He has served as an advisor to multiple presidents and as honorary chairman of the 2015 National Day of Prayer.

"I can't think of two more dynamic people than Todd and Penni Graham. Through this book, their inspirational story will teach people about how to be successful. It will reveal the importance of surrounding yourself with great people and taking care of the people that have helped you make it in life."

Mike Case, founder and president of Case & Associates Properties, Inc. has contributed to numerous nonprofits and philanthropic causes.

"This work will blow your mind with interesting behind the scene stories, facts you'll want to know and for sure impact the way you positively do life."

Tony Jeary, The RESULTS Guy™, is a husband, proud father, prolific author, results coach, and strategist who is blessed to be an encourager to thousands around the globe. His track record includes writing more than 50 books and personally coaching the presidents of Walmart, SAMs, Ford, Samsung, American Airlines, New York Life and many of the world's other high achievers

"Todd and Penni Graham's story is a great story of accomplishment. It's a story of courage. It's a story of grit. It's a story of hard work and being true to yourself and true to your beliefs even when things are at their bleakest. This book will help people understand how to deal with adversity and difficult change. It will encourage people to never lose their faith and to stay true to their commitments."

Bill Kent's family of companies includes Kent Lubrication Centers, Arizona Kent Lubrication Centers, Inc., Professional Lube Management, Inc., Wescon Management Group, Inc., KF Financial, LLC, Kent Tire Company, and Team Kent Motorsports. Bill has been recognized for his outstanding philanthropic endeavors by national organizations.

"Todd and Penni Graham are a formative team. Reading their stories in this book will help people understand the importance of hard work, having a positive attitude, and keeping the faith."

Bucky Allshouse is a trustee of Rice University and one of Texas's leading attorneys, who has been involved with the Rice community almost continuously since his graduation, serving on the Board of Governors and as past president of the "R" Association, the Owl Club, and Alumni Association.

"I enjoyed being around Todd and Penni because—and this is as simple as I can put it—what you see is what you get. Barry Switzer once said, and I'm sure somebody said this before him, that some people are born on third base and think they hit a triple. Todd wasn't born on third base. But factoring in where he started and where he finished, he hit a grand slam. And being around Penni was always joyful. She's my Mount Rushmore of coaches' wives."

Jimmie Tramel, a former Oklahoma sports writer of the year, has written books about former Oklahoma football coach Barry Switzer and former Oklahoma State football coach Pat Jones. Jimmie is a pop culture and feature writer at the *Tulsa World*. His insights and encyclopedic mind create original and entertaining reading.

"The Graham story is a sweet story. Their story is real. Through their life, they've always been candid and frank about what they've done right and what they've done wrong, and through that they've continued to evolve and improve. They always learn from their mistakes and laugh at themselves and get up the next morning with that tenacity and persistence to go out and live in the moment better than they did the day before with the mindset that they're going to change their corner of the world."

Jack Furst is the founder and chairperson of Oak Stream Investors. Jack is an advisor for multiple corporations and serves on numerous boards. As president of The Furst Family Foundation, Jack has been named Outstanding Philanthropist for his enormous support of the Boy Scouts of America and Arizona State University.

"One of the most important lessons in life is responding to adversity. That's what Tenacious is all about. It's about always being positive and always sticking together no matter what. The stories and principles laid out in this book will be inspirational and a great encouragement to anyone who reads it."

Bo Graham is a former D-1 football coach and player. In an integral role on Coach Todd Graham's staff, Bo aided in Todd's successes as a coach at Rice, Tulsa, Pittsburgh, and Arizona State.

"I've watched Todd and Penni Graham grow up. I've watched the transitions in their life with their family and the road they cut out for themselves in the college game. Because I know their story so well, I know that if you pick up this book that you're fixing to read something that's going to impact your life. It will improve your relationships and help you deal with change."

Duke Sparks is completing his fiftieth year in secondary education where he has served as a teacher, coach, head coach, assistant principal, and principal. In addition, Duke was the directory of football operations at Rice University for Head Coach Todd Graham.

"The energy between two people is supernatural and creates great teams, marriages, and legendary results! The wisdom of Proverbs tells us that this is because two are better than one. My friends Penni and Todd Graham are a great embodiment of this, and you'll be blessed by reading about their journey and timeless lessons."

Bob Beaudine, president and CEO of Eastman & Beaudine and bestselling author of *The Power of Who* and *2 Chairs*.

OUR PLAYMAKERS

Dedicated to Our Children

When the Student Becomes the Master

Being your mom is the greatest gift of my life. You gave me more than I can ever describe. You gave me purpose, perspective, forgiveness, hope, and most of all, faith. When you each were born, I was never happier, but watching you become adults and seeing your amazing hearts and gifts and accomplishments makes every day magical for me. Friends and family always comment on how you care for each other, your sensitivities to those around you, and your love and compassion. You have shown me how to be more compassionate and loving and that being a giver is the best gift.

I admit to feeling regret sometimes, wishing I could have given you a fantasy childhood; I know the challenges you faced sometimes, but your tumbles made you stronger and smarter and more empathic. If our life had been a pervasive peace, it would have been boring, and we would not have these lessons to share.

Know that I am proud of each of you—of your accomplishments and achievements, but more importantly, of who you have become in life: not what you do, but who you are. You have shown me how to love people unconditionally and opened my heart and mind, while also having healthy boundaries. Much of what I share in this book you lived through, and I learned through you.

Love you,
Mom

Tenacious

Published by Clovercroft Publishing, Franklin, Tennessee

Edited by OnFire Books

Cover Photography by Stephanie Heymann

Copy Editing, Cover and Interior Design by Adept Content Solutions

Printed in the United States of America

978-1-950892-05-1

CONTENTS

1 TENACIOUS CHARACTER

2 TENACIOUS SMART

3 TENACIOUS DISCIPLINE

4 TENACIOUS TOUGH

POSTGAME

IT'S MORE THAN A GAME

Todd Graham

FOREWORD

TENACIOUS!

That word says a lot about the way I coach football, the way our family fights through adversity, and the way Penni and I try to live our faith.

You're about to read many stories that will illustrate how tenacity has been a key to every success we've ever experienced. Before you get started, it's important that you understand a few other things about us, starting with how our story began.

Penni and I have very similar backgrounds. We both come from broken families. We both became educators. We both were instilled with a deep desire to impact young people very early in our careers. We both had siblings who endured many hardships with us, creating an inspired bond that motivated us both to achieve success in life. Early on, we learned the importance of family and teamwork and to serve others above yourself.

For me, it was a passion to coach. After my mother, the coaches in my life were the biggest game changers. They gave me a chance to be something better. They inspired a turnaround in my life. For Penni, it was a passion to teach. She had a knack for technology and became one of the most innovative educators in Texas. Penni, in fact, was one of the first teachers to have the internet in her classroom.

In 1995, I took the head coaching job at Allen High School in Texas. I was offered the job after many coaches had shied away from it because the program was at the bottom of 5A football in Texas. At the same time, Penni was one of the rising stars in the school district. With Dr. Barbara Erwin, we played a vital role on a dynamic team that transformed the school district into one of the best in the nation.

My superintendent asked me to go to what they called the Cabinet Leadership Meetings, which were attended by the top administrators in the district. She told me, "I want you to meet Penni. She's integrating technology into the classroom, and there might be some merit to doing that with football."

I wasn't interested. Back then, I had an old-school way of teaching and training. But then I walked into the room and saw her for the first time. I thought to myself, "Oh wow. Maybe this technology stuff isn't so bad."

We quickly developed a synergy that was so different from anything I'd experienced in my life. She was beautiful, smart, and all of that, but I was even more intrigued by her passion, drive, and knowledge. Both of us were really focused on our careers. We weren't educators because we wanted to make a bunch of money. We were educators because we wanted to give back to the kids what had been given to us. Because of our passion for changing others' lives, we connected immediately.

We dated for a long time, and from the time I met her, everything about me improved. I became a better coach. I became a better teacher. I became a better dad. I became a better friend. I became better at everything I was doing.

> One of the most important things I learned from Penni was how to connect with students. Penni has always been a champion of relationships. She's brought the best out of me every day. She's inspired me and motivated me. The success I've had has come from a team effort. Most people that know us would agree with that.
>
> At the end of the day, we're all about relationships. In this endeavor that we took on, our goal has been to be difference makers and dream makers. That's what inspires and motivates us. We want to leave a legacy of service. We want to serve people through not just relationships, but championship relationships.

It wasn't always easy; in fact, most of the time it was very hard. Ironically, before Penni and I got married, she had never seen a college football game in person. Four months later, we packed up when I took the job as the linebacker coach and co–defensive coordinator at West Virginia University. We both took massive cuts in pay for me to coach college football and moved all the way across the country. We went through a ton of difficulties during that time, but it was also the time when we grew the most.

Those difficulties and other challenges we faced over the years prepared us for one disappointing event in particular: after a successful six-year run at Arizona State University, the administration decided not to renew my contract. I didn't see it coming. My closest friends didn't see it coming.

In that moment, I had two choices: make excuses, lashing out in anger, or be thankful and respond graciously. It was tough. It was the first time I'd been fired anywhere. I had hoped to stay at ASU for years to come. But Penni really helped me get through it. In fact, she helped me write the speech that I gave at a press conference on November 26, 2017. Here are a few portions of that speech:

This is my life's work, and I have a full heart; I have a full heart today. I'm just so grateful for the opportunity and the blessings. I am a blessed man, no question about it, and I want to thank them for that. Six years ago, coming in here, it was a very different place, and you always want to leave a place better than you found it, and I really feel like we've done that. …I'm just really proud of what we've done to instill student-athletes back into this place and what that means. I walked in here, and we had a 2.2 GPA (in 2012), and that does mean a lot to me. We're at a 3.0 GPA, and we're doing what we should do for young people, and that's helping them get an education. …I'm a Sun Devil, and I think I always will be. A couple of my kids attended here, and one graduated from here. I didn't build this place to tear it down. That's what I told our players today. This place is not about one person. This place is about a set of values and what it means to be a Sun Devil. That's something that's really important to me. …I serve a great God, and I really have a peace about [the decision]. I feel really fortunate and grateful that I had the opportunity to be here. I got up this morning and I opened my Bible up to Proverbs 3:5–6: "Trust in the Lord with all your heart and soul. Don't lean on your own understanding. But in all your ways acknowledge Him and trust Him and He'll make your path straight."

What we wanted to convey through that speech is that football, for us, has always been more than a game. It's a calling. It's a ministry. From the time we met, we've had a fire in us to make a difference. That fire is our faith in God. Penni and I are a dynamic team, but if you take God out of this thing, we are absolutely nothing.

And it's our faith that ignites our souls to love, serve, teach, and inspire others. That's why there's never been much of a line between our family and our football family. Those are our kids.

This book provides a detailed roadmap. Readers will learn the strategies to follow to have a championship life. It's something we've come to call "The Graham Game Plan," and it all starts with our core values: "Character, Smart, Discipline, Tough." From there, it's all about priorities, faith, focus, structure, and execution.

We want our story to inspire all people. It's really for anybody who wants to succeed and live a championship life. And while we don't claim to be perfect or believe that we've arrived, we do know that if you will put your faith in God and your family, then you will have a tenacious championship life.

PLAY BIG

love unconditionally

TEAMWORK

STRIVE TO CONTINUOUSLY IMPROVE

COMMUNICATE DAILY

TENACIOUS JOURNEY

PLAYBOOK

The GRAHAM Game Plan

The Opposition's Strategy

The 7 C's Call Sheet

DO YOU WANT TO SHRINK OR GROW?

INTRODUCTION

This is the question we face daily at work and home. Change is a constant that affects all humans, despite our almost instinctual aversion to it. In this book, I will share stories and lessons showing how my husband, Coach Todd Graham, and I infused programs, people, and places with transformational cultures that focus on winning in all facets of life. This is more than a book; it is guide for a Tenacious Journey. The stories, lessons, and exercises shared in these pages come from an authentic place of both pain and passion, giving the reader tools to overcome obstacles, adapt to changes, and accelerate growth in their personal and professional lives. By writing this book, I hope to make a difference in the lives of others by sharing the strategies and methods Todd and I have discovered in our own Tenacious Journey.

What is the "Tenacious Journey"? It is a way to strengthen the foundations of your life, change your legacy and become your best self.

- Going from Fruitless to Formidable.
- Going from Foolish to Foresight.
- Going from Fractious to Phenomenal.
- Going from Fatigued to Fierce.

Do you want to reach your potential and expand your world? Since you are reading these words, I think you do. We have four features to help you create your future.

1. FOUR CORE VALUES: CHARACTER, SMART, DISCIPLINE, TOUGH

In our Tenacious Journey, we adopted four critical core values: "Character, Smart, Discipline, Tough." Each section of the book concentrates on one of these values. In both sports and life, these four essential values help people succeed and adapt to change. "Character" is the quality inside of you that responds to change happily, even joyfully, and helps other people to behave in the same way. "Smart" is the part of you that responds effectively to change with foresight and adaptability. It is the ability to be smart about cutting through distractions and obstacles to handle tough situations and reach your goals. "Discipline" is the value that lets you execute your plans with commitment and organization. It reflects the order that exists in the world around you. "Tough" is the quality inside of you that helps you achieve long-term goals with short-term resilience. Todd and I have instilled our core values—character, smart, discipline, and tough—within ourselves, our family, and our colleagues at work; these values provide a fundamental foundation for positive change. As you read the narratives of our lives on and off the field, you will learn how to apply these values in order to accelerate your own life.

2. THE GRAHAM GAME PLAN

It is vital for you not to suffer from willful blindness. Do not ignore when you are sick or when your marriage is falling apart. Be willing to make the changes now that will lead you to the life that you want. Using The GRAHAM Game Plan, I will reveal how Goals, Relationship, Agency, Habit, Adventure, and Miracles are keys to opening the doors to your dreams. Building on core values of "Character, Smart, Discipline, Tough," The GRAHAM Game Plan takes a unique approach to strategic planning. The GRAHAM Game Plan creates a new model of transformation addressing not only Goals but also other critical attributes for change: Relationships, Agency, Habits, Adventures, and Miracles.

3. THE OPPOSITION'S STRATEGY

All organizations can learn from the way a football team prepares for game day. Part of the planning is building the best call sheet to exploit the other team's weakness and knowing your own weakness to prevent the opponent from capitalizing on them. Preparing for game day requires the coaches and the players gather three kinds of information:

- **Strengths and weaknesses** of the players and plays from previous games;
- **Strengths and weaknesses** of the new opponent in previous games; and
- **Best strategies** available for the next game based on the success rates of the strategies for previous games of both teams.

Just as the game day plan includes an understanding of the players' deficits, the opposition's strategy must be met to prevent failure in your endeavors. This section lists the feelings and behaviors that will destroy your dreams and lead to misery. These are what keep you prisoner to old ways of thinking, preventing you from writing a new story We need to understand our situation accurately so we can become people who live excellent lives.

4. THE 7 C'S CALL SHEET

By gathering this information, the coaches and the players learn which strategies are the most effective and the least effective, and they choose the most effective strategies for the next game. These plays go on to a call sheet. Using the call sheet, coaches and players can create new plans easily, implementing the plans instantly on the field as the clock approaches 0:00. This is the laminated sheet of paper coaches carry as they walk up and down the field and refer to between plays. If you see it flying into the air, it means the other team is better prepared.

Smart coaches and players tend to win the most games, for they not only find the weaknesses in their opponents' plans but also adapt during the game to exploit these weaknesses. Smart teams are aware their own deficiencies and consistently work to remove them and call sheet includes plays to make the most of the team's skills and abilities.

You will be challenged by The 7 C's call sheet in each section. It calls for you to take action to create your best self. In each section, the 7 C's provide opportunities for you to cultivate your understanding of seven core behaviors and learn new strategies for applying them to grow personally and professionally.

The 7 C's Call Sheet behaviors include:

♥ **Compassionate.**

◉ **Connected.**

♛ **Commanding.**

🤝 **Courageous.**

🔗 **Creative.**

✦ **Committed.**

📍 **Captivating.**

DO NOT BE COMMON

Change is happening faster than ever in today's world, and it affects each of us in different ways—spiritually, mentally, physically, and emotionally. Todd and I have learned that we can either react to change positively and thrive in it or react negatively and let it crush us. Neither Todd nor I ever expected to thrive. We have both experienced at least seven of the ten Adverse Childhood Experiences (ACEs)[1] indicators of childhood trauma, which correlate with many negative complications—ranging from all kinds of impairments to poor decision-making and even death.[2] Todd and I have both made mistakes. We have created some pretty awful narratives in our heads over the years. However, we have chosen

---

[1] According to the ten-question Adverse Childhood Experiences Questionnaire, as used by the National Council of Juvenile and Family Court Judges (https://www.ncjfcj.org/sites/default/files/Finding%20Your%20ACE%20Score.pdf).

[2] See The CDC's "ACE Pyramid." (https://www.cdc.gov/violenceprevention/childabuseandneglect/acestudy/about.html)

to define our pasts not by what they were, but by what we have learned that:

- We are God's wonderful, original pieces of art.
- Other people's feelings are not our responsibility.
- The things we think and learn are our choices.
- Understanding and valuing other people's thoughts and opinions is a sign of respect.
- Carrying any grudge can only hurt us.
- Children will teach us humility, and for that we are grateful.
- Real relationships last for decades, so a bad year or two is not so awful.
- We should make an effort to laugh and smile as much as we did when we were children.
- We should give everything to God.
- Be a light that shines and shares His grace.
- The world does not define us.
- Our pasts do not define who we are now or in the future. We have been able to share these lessons with friends, family, organizations and corporations. Now, we are sharing them with you. I hope some of these lessons of failure and success benefit you and help you live the life you desire.

CHANGE YOUR LEGACY

Todd says, "We're going to create young men who are givers, not takers, who are bright-eyed, not dull-eyed, who are victors, not victims, who are basically in the service of others. We want young people who value their academics, who are smart, who see themselves as smart, and who have discipline."

Todd and I both have a passion for making positive change the legacy of as many people and organizations as we can. We are so grateful for all the people who invested their time and energy to create incredible opportunities for us. We experienced incredible turnarounds in our lives. As a college football coach, Todd had teams that experienced miraculous turnarounds on and off the field, reaching levels of success they had not experienced in decades. Individual players gained new levels of success and numerous academic, character, and athletic honors and awards. Todd has coached three teams to the biggest turnarounds in NCAA Division 1 football. As a result, he was recognized as the 2006 C-USA and 2013 Pac-12 Coach of the Year.

This statement from Mike Case shows the impact Todd had on programs:

> "Todd took our program to another level. He generated excitement, and he came up with high-octane football that everyone loved. Todd understood the game and would put every ounce of his effort forward to be successful. He did a heck of a job."

As a coach's wife, I also have an intimate knowledge of college football. I bring that knowledge and combine it with my experience as an elite educator and successful businesswoman, along with my postgraduate work and certifications, which informed me about multiple aspects of strategic planning, psychology, leadership, learning, resilience, change, and the future of community. I also have the objectivity necessary to share stories of the transformations Todd and I have experienced in our lives. Some of our transformations took place in the years before we met, but the lion's share of our journey of change has occurred in the twenty years since then. As you read, we hope that you are inspired to become Tenacious about transforming your world so you too can leave a positive legacy in your life, your family, and your community.

> "It's been awesome," our son Bo Graham says, "and I know we've made a major positive impact on the lives of so many people over the years. I am grateful that I was able to be a part of our football family, which is my dad's and Penni's legacy."

PARALLEL LIVES

Todd and I were both born into storms of adversity. Although the storms were great, our dreams and determination to make a difference were greater. By the grace of God, a lot of hard effort, and the support of many wonderful people, our lives have been transformed, and we've emerged into a big, beautiful place.

Todd and I were born only eight months apart and had very similar childhoods. Even though we didn't meet until we were thirty, we share much of the same history and even some of the same memories. As we look back, we marvel at how our paths veered so close together at times before we met, and we're even more amazed at the providential way our paths eventually crossed and, through many changes, were intertwined into one. God had great plans for us—together.

What follows is the story of our transformations and the Tenacious Journey God has led us through.

BEING A COACH'S KID

Nothing is stronger in parents' hearts than the overwhelming desire to protect their children. But those blessed to be the parents of coaches' kids know we cannot protect them from everything. Coaches' kids know that their parents' jobs are uncertain. Our kids grew up not knowing if we would be in the same town the following school year (we moved more times than any of us cares to remember) and enduring the fallout of wins and losses as much as any of the players.

> Through it all, our six children—Bo, our coach; Natalie, our entrepreneur; Hank, our engineer; Haylee, our registered nurse; Dakota, our philosopher; and Michael, our student athlete—bore burdens they did not ask for with grace, dignity, and courage.

When Todd and I got married, we had five kids between us, most of them pretty young—a four-year-old, a fifth grader, a sixth grader, a seventh grader, and a senior in high school. Then two years later, we had Michael. One of my biggest challenges in raising five and then six children was letting go of my perfect family scenario. I was stressed because we could never give our kids everything they wanted. But as a result, they've learned so much and are fully independent and capable young adults. Our kids haven't had an easy life by any stretch of the imagination, but they were all born with great skill sets.

Our family is a fun, diverse group of people we truly enjoy. They're all very different, but how blessed we are! Even though I didn't feel I was a successful parent most of the time, I can look at the

e moving to WVU, Graham was a highly-
l high school coach and athletic direc-
n High School for six years (1995-2000).
s made five playoff appearances and
bi-district championships. In 2000,
ted a 9-3 record and captured a Class
n II bi-district title, defeating four
ked among the top-10 in Texas.
ously, Gra-
the head
at Carl

outcome. We have six kids who are smart, beautiful, and wonderfully made. They are all healthy, care about people, and have great relationships. Five of them are even college graduates. How amazing! Now I do not think any family comes close to perfection. I've had to learn in all my relationships to appreciate the whole person and love them at all times, even when there are things I might not want or like. Sometimes we need to step back and observe a person as a work of art. When we do, we can see how wonderful they are, in spite of things about them that frustrate us. Their warts and all—just like our own—are part of the whole beautiful work of art.

We learned a huge lesson about our children: we cannot change them. The only people we can truly change are ourselves. We learned that we can be there to give advice when they ask for it and that we can guide them and support them in healthy ways, but they are ultimately in God's hands. Of course, we had some major challenges as our children were growing up. All families do.

Our kids made some mistakes, and we made some mistakes, and these mistakes created conflict over the years. One piece of wisdom a friend gave me when my daughter was going through a period of "hating" me is that the relationship between parent and child is at least a fifty-year relationship. This perspective allowed me to take a breath and know I had not lost my daughter. In fact, soon after, my daughter and I had the relationship I had longed for. This is a lesson I have passed on to other parents hundreds of times.

I can look back now and see how many of my prayers were answered over time. But instead of enjoying my family during this time of waiting, I walked around in fear and shame, because I could not be the perfect mom. Life was not meeting my expectations. The truth, though, was that my kids did not want a perfect mom. They wanted a present mom. Had I learned to treasure what I had at the time, I would have been a much better person, wife, mother, family member, and friend.

Bo, Natalie, Hank, Haylee, Dakota, and Michael: you all are wonderful. We are proud to be your parents and cannot wait to see what God has in store for each of you on your magnificent journeys.

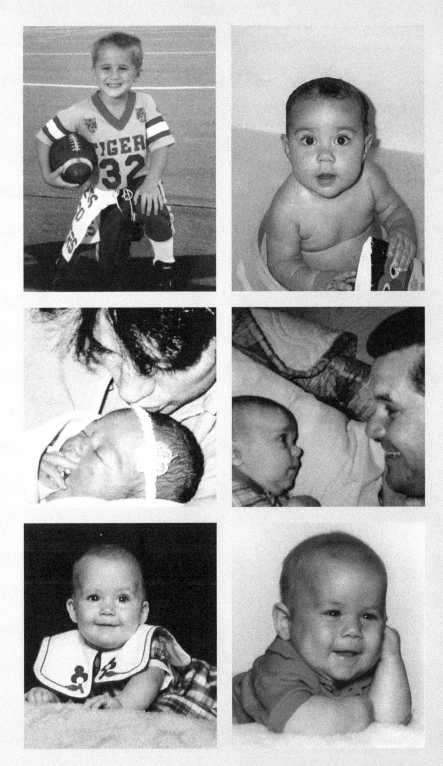

TEAMWORK

CELEBRATE!
RECOGNIZE
DIVERSE TALENTS

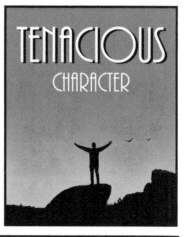

TENACIOUS
CHARACTER

LAUGH & ENJOY
THE JOURNEY

HAVE AN
ATTITUDE
OF
GRATITUDE

PLAYBOOK

The GRAHAM Game Plan

Opposition's Character Strategy

The Character Call Sheet: 7 C's

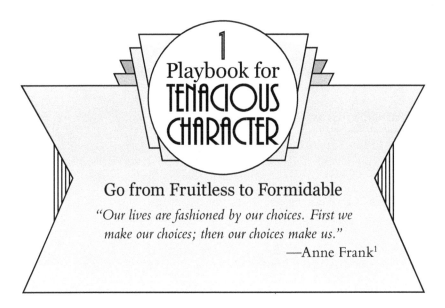

1

Playbook for TENACIOUS CHARACTER

Go from Fruitless to Formidable

"Our lives are fashioned by our choices. First we make our choices; then our choices make us."

—Anne Frank[1]

LIVING ON SAND

Once we built a house on sand. ... Living on sand fills you with fear, because you do not know which tide might take you away. You stand at risk of the tides of insecurity, distrust, anxiety, negativity, promises not kept, or lack of a tribe to love, learn from, or protect you. You focus only on remaining in place—standing still—while envy and frustration grow as you look longingly at the houses built on rock. In a house built on sand, our self-doubt increases, and our self-respect weakens. At times, all of us go through this sandy life. Fear keeps us from developing tenacious character.

A HOUSE BUILT ON ROCK

The people who live in houses built on rock have tenacious character. Each of them lives according to the core values of truth, commitment, gratitude, love of service, and a willingness to sacrifice for others, and they have relationships filled with communication, authenticity, and appreciation. Houses built on rock—the core values—can withstand any storms that may come their way.

---

[1] Anne Frank, *Anne Frank's Tales from the Secret Annex*, trans. Susan Massotty (New York: Bantam Dell, 1982).

The GRAHAM Game Plan for Tenacious Character

GOAL: Become a character advocate.

RELATIONSHIP: Identify and know yourself.

AGENCY: Grow your personal power.

HABITS: Surround yourself with people of great character.

ADVENTURE: Build a culture of character.

MIRACLE: Making heavenly connections.

Opposition's Character Strategy

Keep your life full of *fear*.

Feed on *negativity*.

Fear change or being different and unique.

Instill a *"victim"* mentality.

Weaken your sense of *self control*.

Make you a *chameleon,* changing to fit your environment instead of being your authentic self.

Feel *envy* and *coveting*.

Show *bigotry* and *bias*.

Feel *loneliness*.

Develop *bad habits* that harm yourself or those who love you.

Have a sense of *entitlement* or a feeling that you are owed something.

Weaken your internal *motivation*.

THE CHARACTER CALL SHEET: 7 C'S

1. Be Compassionate.
Chip away the marble to show your authentic self.
Have gratitude.

2. Be Captivating.
Live in the present.

3. Be Commanding.
Identify what you cannot control.
Break free.
Lead by example.

4. Be Committed.
Make a mask to delegate negative thoughts.

5. Be Connected.
Keep oaths to yourself.
Expand your world.
Start connections.

6. Be Courageous.
Define how you are unique.

7. Be Creative.
Plan your life.
Start a culture of strong character.
Adaption actions.

GOAL: BECOME A CHARACTER ADVOCATE

Develop and appreciate strong character in yourself and others. Character means loving and serving others and yourself. Developing your physical, emotional, mental, and spiritual health is essential to living a life of character. Knowing who you are and your gifts are quintessential to building strong character. You cannot be a giver if you have nothing to give.

Living by your core values provides you and others the rudder to guide your ship. Respecting others and yourself, operating in ethical manner and with integrity, taking responsibility for your actions and bringing a positive attitude to all that you do and encouraging others to do the same promotes a culture of strong character. Still, character is a broad term. I think the best definition of character can be found in the Bible: "The fruit of the Spirit is love, joy, peace, forbearance, kindness, goodness, faithfulness, gentleness and self-control" (Galatians 5:22–23).

Character requires the understanding that each person is unique and authentic. We are alive for a very short amount of time, so we need to appreciate the scarce time we have together. Strength of character determines how well we live. We have many tribes—at work, at church, in our communities, at school, and at home. All tribes are made up of individuals. Building a tribe of character starts with you. You need to know the truth about who you are and where you are going.

RELATIONSHIP: IDENTIFY AND KNOW YOURSELF

There is no "awesome" without *me*! A tenacious life takes you on a journey through both mountains and valleys. If you want to grow and experience the most life has to offer, you must first know that life is about your choices. Your journey starts with you. To get to your destination, you must first know who you are. By defining your values, personality, and identity, you can better understand where you want to go and what you have packed in your bag. To do this, you need to control your feelings and thoughts and have a healthy relationship with yourself and others.

The beautiful thing about football is that each player gains a strong sense of identity, and with that identity comes pride. Every player brings pride to the team when he helps bring the team to victory, and every triumph brings pride to the school. I loved the experience of feeling proud for my team, regardless of which team Todd coached.

However, I realized that I was living a pattern many people fall into: I was my job. My identity was what I did or how others defined me. I had to end my career because of the frequent moves and the responsibilities of Todd's head coaching career. Outside of football, I had no sense of identity, no sense of belonging. I longed for my old identity. No longer did I experience the appreciation and validation I had in the workplace. I was happy to spend more time at home with my kids and be the support system for my husband and his team. Michael and I spent most of our days at Rice University, where I tried to do whatever was needed. They had a small staff and few resources.

I discovered the benefit of creating time for myself instead of letting other people control my time. I had to explore my identity outside the workplace. I firmly believe there is power in knowing your identity. I envy people who have a strong sense of cultural identity, because a strong identity brings with it a strong voice, a sense of belonging. Since my family is so spread out, I grew up without a strong family cultural identity, and in Texas, your family identity is everything.

If someone had put out a BOLO (Be On the Look Out) on me, officers would have rolled their eyes: average height, weight, hair color, eye color, and nothing distinguishing. On the one hand, this has been a blessing in my life, because my identity became whatever other people needed. I developed the skill of morphing so that I could fit in with almost any group. On the other hand, I lacked an inner core of my own identity, so I felt like I was living a fake life. I was always an authentic person, but I consistently lacked confidence and a sense of self-worth.

Not only was I letting others define me, but my cultural heritage was also full of secrets. In Texas, for the most part, people want to know your nationality. My nationality was a constant source of both myth and mystery. From what I knew, most of my family had been in Texas before the United States existed as a country, and some of my family had been in Texas before it was the Republic of Texas. There were many family secrets that I was unaware of. I thought from family lore that I had strong Native American roots, as well as Jewish and some African American heritage. When we were in Jerusalem, I felt a deep connection with "my people." After studying Texas history and knowing where various Native American tribes settled, I had decided I was Comanche because they had settled in an area from which part of my family originated. However, through DNA testing, I found out that I was almost 100 percent British and Northern European. I was disappointed. I had loved my myths. However, the test revealed no Jewish or Native American DNA and only enough African American DNA to come from Adam and Eve. I have learned that my family arrived in Tennessee around 1600 and in Texas around 1780. The only cultural traditions I knew were Texan, so the identity I decided to claim is Texan. I now have an answer when people ask about my heritage.

When people ask about my family, my description sounds like a very long Jeff Foxworthy redneck joke. We could easily have a dozen Maury Povich or Dr. Phil shows on our family lineage. I have a family orchard, not a tree. When my kids did their family tree posters in third grade, I just wanted to write the word "Complicated" across the top. No poster board was large enough to capture three generations, let alone five. This family orchard added another layer of complexity to my identity.

Finding Your Masterpiece

From my studies, I know that having a sense of identity helps us regulate our emotions, handle difficult situations calmly, connect with others more fluidly, act more independently, and build healthier relationships. Although my identity developed through my increased self-awareness after years of learning, education, and counseling, friends and family also helped me define who I am. Then I realized that I am a masterpiece of God. Recognizing this led me to the tenacious pursuit of finding my true identity. I learned what I am supposed to do and what God's purpose is for me. I am also grateful for all the tools we used in staff development to help us define our values, strengths and weaknesses, and core personality types.

Here are some tools you can use to discover how God has made you a living masterpiece:

Values Inventory
Myers-Briggs Personality Description
DISC Assessment Description

Values Inventory

Do you know what your core values are? Your core values determine your journey and the success of your organization. Do you feel a deep longing for the future? Defining and living your ideal core values will take you where you want to be. Usually, the key to going from where you are to where you want to be, is having a map that leads you to the roads with the right values, then not taking any detours.

First, you must examine the ways you are living now and how your actions show your core values. When you look at how you spend your time and money, you can identify some of your core values.

Step One:
Describe how you use your time:

What does you daily routine look like?
What do you do with your free time?

Describe how money functions in your life:

How you earn your money?
What you do with your money?

Step Two:
Reflect on the 7 C's. Define your behaviors, feelings, and actions to compare to the core value list.

When do you act **C**ourageous?
How and to whom are you **C**ommitted?
For whom do you show **C**ompassion?
To what or to whom do feel **C**onnected?
Where and how do you take **C**ommand?
What **C**aptivates you?
Where and how do you feel the most **C**reative?

Step Three: Define your current core values.
Make a list of your current core values based on answers from steps one and two. Go to https://corevalueslist.com for examples of more than 500 core values.

Step Four: Examine the list of core values.
Make a list of your top ten core values. Get input from colleagues, peers, and family by asking them to select what they think are your top five core values.

Step Five: Based on their input, determine your top three core values.

Step Six: After reading the rest of *Tenacious*, come back to the Values Inventory. Go through steps one through five, based on where you want to go and what you want your core values to be.

After determining your new core values, you will have a new map to lead you to the roads with the right values. Use the tools in *Tenacious* to keep yourself going the right direction.

Values Keep Us Grounded

"What I think Todd brings to the table, [is that] he lives his life without compromise, in a world in which there is so much compromise of integrity and values," said Pastor Jack Graham.

You want to have strong relationships and strong character. To achieve your goals, you must be led by commitment to your core values. The right values build healthy workplaces, communities, homes, and selves. These values propel us toward the right goals, helping both people and organizations to be better. Selecting the right values is critical to our success. Circumstances will always change, because life is filled with change. Our core values help us respond to change in ways that benefit everyone, including ourselves. If we lack core values, then it is likely that our response to change will be unhealthy and possibly destructive to ourselves and others. If we hold on to our core values tenaciously, despite massive changes, then we develop a center of gravity that helps us navigate to safety in whatever storm we find ourselves.

Myers-Briggs Personality

Myers-Briggs asks four questions:

1. Are you outwardly or inwardly focused? People who answer "outward" tend to be extroverts and love socializing. People who answer "inward" tend to be introverts and love thinking deeply about things and exploring their emotions. I or E
2. How do you prefer to take in information? People who pay attention to facts and reality as it exists now tend to rely on data they can sense. People who look at the big picture and see possibilities tend to rely on their intuition. S or N
3. How do you prefer to make decisions? People who use logic tend to prefer thinking. People who focus on personal values tend to prefer feeling. T or F
4. How do you prefer to live your outer life? People who live by rules and deadlines tend to use judgment. People who prefer

flexibility and open options tend to prefer perceiving the world in different ways. J or P

DISC

Another tool for personality assessment is DISC. As originally developed by William Moulton Marston, DISC stands for Dominance, Inducement (Influence), Submission (Steadiness), and Compliance (or Conscientiousness). According to Marston, all of these personality types exist in every person and emerge in various environments.[2]

Someone who is dominant wants to be in control most of the time. This person wants to be the team captain, the chairman of the board, the leader of the company, the decision-maker. Someone who wants influence is a great cheerleader or a great coach, encouraging people to give praise for the team effort. Someone who is steady (submissive or supportive) tends to notice and tend to people's needs. Finally, someone who is conscientious knows that there are regulations to obey, rules to follow, details to master. This person makes sure all the proper forms are completed on time.

We are diverse. It is part of the reality we must understand. We all have our own reactions and feelings. The distinctiveness of each person helps us solve problems and find the best solution, as long we respect each others' differences and make the most of our strengths.

 **How Are You Unique?**

- How do you define yourself?
- Who decides how you spend your time?
- Where does your energy go?
- How do you spend your time and money?
- With whom do you spend time daily, weekly, or monthly?
- What are your passions and skills?
- Do your passions and skills match how you spend your time and money?
- Do your passions and skills match your relationships?
- What are your personality traits based on your core values, knowledge, Myers-Briggs, and DISC Assessments?

---

[2] It should be noted that Marton's original DISC acronym has been greatly expanded by subsequent researchers and is now known as DiSC®, a trademark of Wiley/Inscape Publishing. https://www.onlinediscprofile.com/what-is-disc/disc-history/

AGENCY: GROW YOUR PERSONAL POWER

You can do anything. Our daughter, Natalie, shares her life lesson.

"What if I told you that you are your only limitation? That literally everything is within reach, but you are the only thing holding you back?" asked my professor.

I had a spectacular professor tell me this when I was in my first year of college. I had approached him for an opinion on whether it was a bad idea to start my first business before I had finished school. He was a generally cold but very logical person, and he knew that I was, well … a work-better-busy type. I had bounced the idea off family and friends, and the general response was that it was not a great idea. People told me to wait on following that dream and to stick it out with the corporate job that was draining my every brain cell.

I chose to ask him because he had none of the emotional attachment or fears that came with familial responses and I knew that if I got that final no, I would probably just bite the bullet and stay on course because I was too insecure to make that decision for myself at the time.

His response was, as expected, an unemotional one, but one that created an enormously emotional response in me.
When I asked and he responded with that question, it almost seemed like a humorously obvious fact that I had somehow missed. I didn't have a response. Dumbfounded, I thanked him and walked away. How different my life would be today if I hadn't asked him, or if he provided a different, more cautionary response. So, consider this your permission to do anything and everything you set your mind to. With one caveat: you just have to be willing to do the work."

 **Chip Away the Marble**

The great artist Michelangelo wrote, "The sculptor arrives at his end by taking away what is superfluous."[3] Or, as it is put more popularly, "I saw the angel in the marble and carved until I set him free."

Most of us carry extra marble around with us. It needs to be chipped away. Part of loving yourself is chipping away to reveal your championship self.

We make many choices that cause us to remain trapped in marble:

- Do you reflect your environment or affect your environment?
- Can you choose to be happy or not?
- How do you react to hard times in your life—with hope or helplessness?
- Do you take responsibility for your actions or blame others for your failures?
- What choices are you making in your life? Are they the ones that result in positive consequences?

Fear and insecurity in identity lead to struggles with self and relationships. The most important relationship you need to have is with yourself. Imagine seeing a football field, but instead of being rectangular, it is round, and the lines overlap each other. The goal post shifts every few minutes, and you cannot get the players on the field to stay in formation. This is how anxiety, trauma, worry, and negative self-talk can affect our view of the world. It can blur your reality. How can you even get your team lined up if your view of the field is so distorted? How can you have great relationships with anyone if you do not have one with yourself?

By taking off the mask of negative thoughts, mastering the circles of control, keeping promises, and breaking free, I am able to see people and relationships with clear eyes and an open heart.

Strategies for loving yourself:

Mask Making: Compartmentalizing Worry and Anxiety
Circles of Control
Oath to Myself
Escaping My Prison

---

[3] Duppa, Richard, and Quatremere de Quincy, *The Lives and Works of Michael Angelo and Raphael*, London: Bell & Daldy, 1872.

Mask Making: Compartmentalizing Worry and Anxiety

We can control our thoughts and feelings, but it is hard to stop respond-ing to life circumstances immediately with the same negative thoughts. Why is that? Because we're so used to doing it that we get stuck and are unable to change. So I created an imaginary mask of negative thoughts and started setting a time each-day to put on the mask. At 4 p.m. each day, I set a timer and spent five minutes with the mask on, letting all of those negative thoughts—self-doubt, worry, and anxiety—blur my sight. It is a mask because negative thoughts and feelings are not real. You are an amazing gift to this world. Pessimism is learned. Removing the mask enables our true character to be revealed.

When those thoughts started to invade my space during other times of the day, I said, "Remember! I am putting on that mask at 4 p.m." By designating this time, instead of having the mask of negative thoughts on twenty-four hours a day, seven days a week, I limited the negative thoughts to only five minutes. Eventually, a specific time for the mask of negative thoughts was needed only in situations and times of high stress. Assigning a specific time for my negative thoughts not only allowed me to be more present, but also let my worries stay small and compartmentalized, instead of growing and taking over my vision of the world.

 ## Circles of Control

As a tribal leader, I tried to micromanage everyone and everything in our "village," especially my most important bigwigs—our children. I worried and feared that we would be attacked, or they would not have everything they needed for the next season. I could work 24/7 and never do enough. I wanted perfection for everyone and everything. I spent all my time running around the village, missing the joy of the tribe. What really hurt was missing the time to have intimate relation-ships with all the tribal members (my family) because I wasn't present. I learned an elephant-size lesson. The only person I can truly change and control is myself. I couldn't be perfect, much less create perfection for everyone else. This realization filled the village with laughter and entertainment and the village ran smoothly. By focusing on what I had control over, I was able to diminish not only my anxiety, fear, and frus-tration, but that of the other members of my tribe and family as well.

Circles of Control

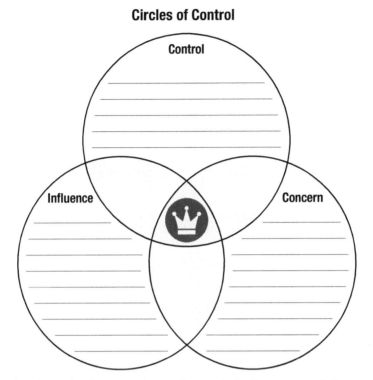

The circles in the graphic are **Control**, **Influence**, and **Concern**.

First Ring (Control): This is the ring of things that we have *control* over.

Second Ring (Influence): This is the ring of things that we have concerns about and can potentially *influence*.

Third Ring (Concern): This is the ring of things that we have *concerns* about, but we cannot control.

Make a list inside each circle.

Keys to be an effective tribal leader:

- **Identify** what you have no control over
- **Grieve** what you must let go
- **Live** in the present
- **Know** the seasons of life that impact our control, influence, and concern
- **Plan** your life
- **Have** gratitude

Saying the Serenity Prayer every day reminds your brain about what it can control. I love the full version. "God grant me the serenity to accept the things I cannot change; courage to change the things I can; and wisdom to know the difference." (Although known most widely in its abbreviated form above, the entire prayer reads as follows: "Living one day at a time; enjoying one moment at a time; accepting hardships as the pathway to peace; taking, as He did, this sinful world as it is, not as I would have it; trusting that He will make all things right if I surrender to His Will; that I may be reasonably happy in this life and supremely happy with Him forever in the next."[4]

Oath to Myself

A few years ago, I wrote my purpose for the year: "to keep promises to myself." Keeping promises to myself has been one of the most important efforts to my personal growth. Usually, I tried to exceed expectations whenever I made promises to someone else, but I never tried to do this for myself. By learning to keep promises to myself, I discovered wants and needs that had been invisible. If someone did not keep promises, I thought it was disrespectful. No one was more disrespectful to me than me. By respecting myself, I became a stronger and happier person, which improved all my relationships.

How can we expect others to respect or keep promises to us, when we can't keep them to ourselves?

Escaping My Prison

Not all of us can let go of the bad things that happen to us, especially when we have no control over what has happened. Many times, we carry around bad memories. Our brains love to hold on to them more than positive memories because bad memories are usually filled with deep emotions. Sometimes, our minds even make a lousy memory worse than the event actually was. Like planting a seed in your mind,

---

[4] While frequently attributed to Reinhold Niebuhr, the original authorship of this prayer, popularized in Alcoholics Anonymous meetings, is unclear. cf. Webb, Terry. *Tree of Renewed Life: Spiritual Renewal of the Church Through the Twelve-Step Program.* New York: Crossroad, 1992.

it just grows. There are times we may even experience sadness or anxiety and think it is caused by external circumstances, when they might be bad memories hanging around in your brain. What do you do with your bad memories? Whether you are aware of it or not, your bad memories may be preventing you from enjoying life. Bad memories can be like a prison, locking us away from the fullness of life.

I had lived with bad memories that were decades old. Unknowingly, these bad memories affected my decision-making and left me with post-traumatic stress disorder.

I lived in Iran. Not a small town in Texas, but the country. Why? When I was nearly thirteen years old, my father's job with AT&T took him to Tehran, Iran, shortly before the Iranian Revolution in 1978. We were supposed to be there three years, but demonstrations against the Shah's reign had started the year before. There were over 40,000 Americans living in Tehran at the time. Our American school had multiple teams playing American football against each other in the fall, I adapted to the five daily calls to prayer that sounded like screaming over the loudspeaker. We did not live within an American community. Our apartment was on Pahlavi, a major road that led to the Shah's palace. The road had four lanes and was always busy. On September 8, 1978, the day before I turned thirteen, the government and protesters had a disastrous conflict in the middle of Tehran. The battle was named "Black Friday" because the military killed thousands of demonstrators. The Shah enacted martial law, and the government and rebel forces began clashing nightly on Pahlavi, in front of my house. My family went out for pizza the night before "Black Friday" to celebrate my birthday. That was the last time my baby brother and I left the house until we got on a plane in December to return to the United States.

I was left without a community. The TV only showed propaganda. I think I was so overcome with the fear of the unknown that most of those months are erased from my memory. At nighttime, we heard the tanks rolling down Pahlavi toward the demonstrators, who were congregating in large groups, wearing white sheets and chanting "Death to Americans" in English for the TV cameras. I saw the protesters getting killed as the white sheets turned red following shots by the military. On December 8th, the United States government recommended that all Americans "temporarily relocate." My mother, brother, and I caught one of the last commercial flights out. The Shah left Iran on January 6th, 1979. My dad did not leave for many more months.

It was not the war or the fear that had the most negative impact on my psyche. It was loneliness, having no friends and no one to talk to. It took years for me to understand that I did not come back as the same person. The loneliness stayed with me and returned strongly at times. We rarely discussed our experiences in Iran. Our environment left us with few answers for how to deal with the war and left us in an emotional state that haunted us. Stigma often goes with recognizing and accepting that we have emotional or mental difficulties. When I returned, I was expected to have a smile on my face and share only positive stories. In fact, the stories I told were far from reality. As I told it, our time in Iran was a great adventure; we traveled and were treated with graciousness. Really, we were in the middle of a war, and I was a prisoner of that war for months. It was hard for me to realize the bad memories and sadness were still with me.

 **Break Free**

What is imprisoning you today?
What steps can you take toward freedom?
What triggers your bad memories?

There are many strategies to set yourself free of bad memories. Have you:

- Read books about letting go?
- Looked for spiritual guidance?

I sought counseling. I went to a Christian counselor and did Eye Movement Desensitization and Reprocessing, or EMDR. During EMDR, I found out I was battling the ghosts of my past. I had been completely unaware they were hanging around in my mind and heart and body. Just by remembering and acknowledging my ghosts, they left and cleared my heart, body, and mind. I now look at my life with clear eyes, a clear heart, and a new sense of freedom.

By removing the marble of fear, control, disrespect, and bad memories, the true masterpiece can be revealed. I am still chipping away to find the best possible me. You cannot control everything that happens, but you can know yourself better. By knowing yourself, you can become your best and increase the power and effectiveness of your actions, empowering yourself and others to be extraordinary.

HABIT: SURROUND YOURSELF WITH PEOPLE OF GREAT CHARACTER

Our character is constantly developing because of the many relationships we have with people of great character. Through modeling, these friends teach us about grace, gratitude, love, appreciation, and support.

Learning Grace and Gratitude from Jack Graham

"I've watched him grow to be truly not only a dynamic coach, but a dynamic man. His spiritual development has skyrocketed, and he's added to the depth of his character."
—Pastor Jack Graham

One of the most important relationships in our lives is with the other Grahams, Jack and Deb. Dr. Jack Graham, pastor of Prestonwood Baptist Church in Plano, Texas, is a wonderful friend and major influence in Todd's life. He taught Todd so much about grace, and we are so grateful.

Jack's son Josh played for Todd when he was head coach at Allen High School in Allen, Texas. Jack is a huge sports fan, and he and Todd established a ritual of having breakfast together every Friday. Eventually, their Friday morning breakfasts turned into discussions of faith. Sometimes other people would join them, like Ross Robinson, another pastor who is now a great friend of ours. Todd credits Jack with helping him turn his mind and heart back to the Lord. It took time, but we eventually learned that we needed to experience the full spectrum of grace and freedom God offers. We came to understand that if we were not experiencing all God has to offer, we were losing out on our capacity to live up to our potential and influence others. We learned that everyone is a sinner. Even if they didn't look perfect, I still thought everyone else was perfect and I wasn't. For a long time, I couldn't let go of the bondage of guilt and shame and accept the grace that God has given us all.

In July of 2005, it became more evident than ever that God had put Jack into our lives for a reason. At the time, Todd was defensive coordinator at the University of Tulsa. Just as fall camp was starting, Todd received a call from his mother, Carol, who told him she was ill. Something was wrong with her heart. He jumped on a plane from Oklahoma to his hometown of Mesquite, Texas, and met her at Mesquite Community Hospital, where she had been admitted. She was having trouble breathing and looked like something close to death. Doctors at the hospital were stingy with hope if there was any to be had. They started running tests, the last of which involved injecting dye into her heart and monitoring its movement through blood vessels. After several hours of tension, they came back with the results: there were blockages in all major arteries caused by diabetes, which had been diagnosed fifteen years too late. She lacked insurance, and the doctors said surgery was too risky and too expensive. They were very cold and short with their answers and just seemed to want to get her out the door. They had decided to send her home to die.

Before she was even released, Todd secured a wheelchair, pulled up to the front of the hospital, and got her out of there. He did not know what he was going to do, where he would go, or how he was going to get her help. As the seconds passed, the chances of her having a fatal heart attack crept upwards. We did not have any insurance or resources and were faced with the thought of taking Mom home to die. In that moment, God put it in Todd to call Jack. He had been such a positive spiritual influence, and he was the only person Todd trusted completely. During the phone call, Todd confessed that he was at a loss as to what to do, scared, and hoping Jack would pray for his mother. Jack offered more than a prayer, telling Todd to go to Presbyterian Hospital and exactly to whom he should talk. Without hesitation, Todd and I drove his mom to the hospital.

Carol Graham

Soon after we checked her in, we were visited by Dr. Randall, a thoracic surgeon—in fact, one of the best in the world. The hospital had a completely different atmosphere, receiving us with open arms. Grace was present. Carol was blessed to have the best medical care and doctor possible. And it was all because of Jack Graham. He had called the hospital and arranged everything. Dr. Randall looked at Carol's test results and said that the diagnosis was correct; she should have about a 30 percent chance to live through the surgery. But he said her faith in God would push the percentage up, and that she had to want to get off that table.

The next evening, Carol had surgery. Before the surgery, Todd prayed with Jack and Ross Robinson in the room with Carol and the comfort of the Holy Spirit was put on her heart. The surgery was long but went perfectly, and soon Carol was recovering. When we reached out to the hospital and the surgeon to work out a payment plan, they told us our money was no good and that we had received a blessing from God. The grace we felt and the gratitude for that grace still overwhelms us. It changed us. We saw the power of God and how his grace is always available to all who ask and receive. There are some days I still struggle with receiving that grace, but this period in our lives always reminds me that it is there and available for me—even me.

The Three—Holloway, Clinkscale, Germany—Who
Grew Our Love and Appreciation

From 2007 to 2010, Todd was head football coach at the University of Tulsa, having spent 2006 as head coach at Rice University in Houston. In 2011, he took the position of head football coach at the University of Pittsburgh. That same year, in the space of eight months, three of his former Tulsa players died. They were three of our favorite players, all from the 2007 team. Their names were Wilson Holloway, George Clinkscale, and Anthony Germany, Jr. All of these men were taken during their prime. Why, God?

The week Anthony died, I made a bunch of buttons with the number three on them and handed them out to everyone who would take them at the Pittsburgh Panthers game. People were confused. Even though we were in Pittsburgh, my heart was in Tulsa. I wanted to honor the three players we'd lost.

Wilson Holloway

1. Wilson Hollaway, a man who was always smiling, lost a tough battle with Hodgkin's lymphoma. With his death came a wave of support for his family and friends. Wilson's happiness and humorous attitude were contagious. He fought the disease with a tireless and enthusiastic spirit. While he was on chemo, he was still showing up for practices and class. We'll never forget Wilson's own words, *"I don't take things for granted anymore. There are days I wish I could go out and do the drills everyone hates to do."* Wilson touched all of our hearts with his passion for living. He was

honored for his tenacious spirit with the ESPN Courage Award. He not only beat cancer twice during his time as a college football player, but he also beat out his teammates to win the starting tackle position. After an eleven-win season, he inspired our quarterback, David Johnson, and all the linemen to shave their heads. One month after we left Tulsa, we flew home for Wilson's funeral.

George Clinkscale

2. George Clinkscale had a special place in our hearts. He was a Texan with a big personality. You could hear him laugh a mile away. He played linebacker and started his entire senior year. He had graduated a couple of years earlier and was blessed to have a family. He was an encourager who had pushed himself to be better than anyone else. He left this world suddenly and unexpectedly, which made it especially hard on his family, teammates, and friends, who all loved him dearly. When he died, he was at a charitable event, as anyone who knew him would expect, trying to make other people's lives better.

"Any time I have taken a new job, it has always been challenging for me to leave my current players. I have learned to love them like they are my own and never to take a day for granted with them. We had a player shot and killed on a team that I was coaching, and that event has forced me to become more intentional with speaking truth into my players daily." Coach Trent Figg

Nick Graham and Anthony Germany

3. Anthony Germany won my heart the first time I met him during recruiting. I still cry every time I say his name. He lettered three times at Tulsa and was a starter for two seasons from 2007 to 2010. In June of 2010, he married the love of his life, Chivis. The two had been married a year and a half when Anthony died of complications from a pulmonary embolism in an Oklahoma City hospital on October 18, 2011. Since I was in Pittsburgh at the time, I thought the only thing I could do was gather pictures and memories from teammates, friends, and family and make a memory book as a tribute for his parents, Anthony Sr. and Karon, his wife Chivis, and his dear friend and former TU teammate Nick and Nick's wife Candice, to whose children Anthony had been a godfather. David Johnson wrote in the book:

    "I know 2004 seems like a long time ago when we first came to the University of Tulsa as freshmen striving to play Division 1 college football. One thing that I noticed from the very beginning was your determination and passion for the game of football. You never knew it, but you inspired me and motivated me on a journey of perfection. I enjoyed all the early morning weight sessions with your enthusiastic style of dancing to start the first lift of the day. I considered you as one of my brothers. One that I would fight for every day and one that I highly respected. I love you, brother, and hope you rest easy knowing that you made such a lasting impact on my life and many others that came in contact with you."

These bright young men were taken away from us, and we hope others strive to be like them.

Our peace comes knowing we will see them again, soon.

I know their lives and deaths impacted many. Losing a loved one can have a positive lesson for all of us. As I sat at each celebration of life, I remember how much I appreciated the memories we had. They loved, they gave, and they changed how I was going to live my life.

Nothing on earth can make up for the loss of someone you love, but I can see how it can make us love more deeply and appreciate the moments we have.

These words from Maya Angelou sum up the impact of these young men: *"I've learned that people will forget what you said, people will forget what you did, but people will never forget how you made them feel."*

Jason Wants Us to Be Open and Supportive

I Got You!

Our society does a horrible job of encouraging emotional health. Every family I know has been impacted to some degree emotional or mental illness. This can be seen most significantly in our nation's suicide rate. I have sadly lost people I deeply care about. People do not realize that suicide is the second leading cause of death in the United States for men under the age of thirty-five.[5] In 2018, we lost another friend, former Arizona State Sun Devils football player and Valley TV and radio personality Jason Franklin, to suicide. He was the first person to make you smile, who had beautiful gifts that he shared on and off the field. He was widely loved, but like most people I have known who have taken their own lives, he covered his pain with huge smiles. Many of these people, lacking proper support and help, also make their situations worse by choosing to self-medicate with alcohol and illicit drugs. Of course, with everyone we lose, we wish we could have changed the circumstances.

For that to change, the stigma of mental illness must be challenged. We need to be able to speak openly about what is haunting us. I love how the Franklins chose to celebrate Jason's first year in heaven. As his mother said at the time, "Jason handed the idea to me. As many of you know, one of Jason's favorite sayings was 'I Got You.' He used it all the time for so many positive reasons. So, we have decided to celebrate his birthday's going forward to 'I Got You' days. That is, we will spend the day trying to help others, trying to show them that there are people out there that [have] 'got them' and are there to help get them through their day."

---

[5] https://www.cdc.gov/healthequity/lcod/index.htm

ADVENTURE: BUILD A CULTURE OF CHARACTER

"Todd was heavily invested and just did an outstanding job of persevering and getting the whole stadium and football complex done. He brought an integrity and commitment of character to the entire program."
—Bill Kent

Bo Graham on Changing the Culture of a Football Team

Building a championship culture starts with developing strong championship relationships between everyone involved in the program. Cultivating these types of relationships requires an extraordinary amount of time, effort, and energy. In any team environment, people will only be capable of reaching their full potential as a team once they have forged these strong relationships, built on trust, respect, discipline, and hard work. Reaching the full potential of the team will also require having everyone commit to individual and team goals and to the standards and expectations necessary to achieve those goals.

One of the most important jobs of any football coach is setting this standard and designing a process of accountability, which defines expectations, resulting in the formation of a championship culture. This same model applies across the board: in the classroom, in the community, in the weight room, and on the field. It is the job of coaches and staff to put their athletes in the best positions from which to be successful, both on and off the field. Ultimately, the goal of a coach is to make a positive impact on as many young peoples' lives as possible.

There is nothing more rewarding than working together for one common goal and sharing these successful championship experiences. In order to build a champion, you must be creative and constantly evolving your teaching and motivational methods. You must be innovative and progressive in your ideas and develop a plan that is catered to the skills and talents of the players and coaches you have.

You must also study and know your opponents and build your plan based on what is necessary to beat the best. Competing in everything, we always seek knowledge and improvement, allowing us to sustain championship success. Being able to identify talent early and start that relationship building process is key in your success as a recruiter and is the lifeblood of the program. Players want to compete at the highest level. The best way to quickly attract and recruit the best to your program is to take the players, skills, and talents you have and win right away, showing proof that your program produces highly productive student-athletes year in and year out, regardless of age, background, or position.

One of the greatest challenges in any program is galvanizing these types of championship relationships in very short periods of time. Each season when a team reports for fall camp there are always new faces and every year each team is different and takes on its own personality. When we were at Tulsa, we teamed up each year with GUTS Church and were able to take our teams to Fort Guts located off of Fort Gibson Lake about an hour outside of Tulsa. This was a time when our team ditched their cell phones and participated in team activities day and night.

We also started one of the most valuable traditions in building these types of relationships by having breakout sessions around several campfires at night in order to give our players a chance to tell their stories. We would split up into position groups and each position coach would start by telling his story to his position group of why he coached. Each person was encouraged to share some of their life's greatest challenges and why and for whom they played the game. While at Arizona State University, we were able to bring back the old Sun Devil tradition of Camp Tontozona where our entire operation camped out just outside of Payson, Arizona on the edge of the Tonto National Forest. Every player in the Todd Graham era would first learn the Sun Devil Fight Song and by the end of the week would climb to the top of Mount Kush and sing the fight song with their position group. They would each sign a T-shirt and nail it to the tree of their choice, each year returning to that same spot to renew their commitment just like Jake "The Snake" Plummer and Pat Tillman. It was at these places with very few fans around that the character of our teams were formed. This was the place where our team learned about each other and themselves and formed the types of relationships necessary to compete for championships. Ultimately, how much a team cares about each other depends heavily on the experiences and adversities they face together as a team. By creating this type of environment and getting everyone out of their comfort zones, we were able to forge these types of relationships each and every year. We would like to think that when our former players look back on their careers, it is these types of experiences they remember and cherish the most.

In a world filled with distractions, what are some things you can do with your team to change culture and create a team of strong character? How well do your team members know each other? If you knew what your teammates were fighting for, would you fight harder for them?

Starting a Culture of Strong Character

1. **Change** the environment
2. **Insure** everyone is present: physically, emotionally, and mentally
3. **Build** your team around authentic and meaningful exchanges
4. **Use** breakout sessions to create shared motivations and challenges
5. **Create** traditions that signify a commitment or a renewal of focus for a new season
6. **Reflect** on relationships, commitments, and shared motivations and challenges throughout the season

Building Our Village of Characters

What was true in my childhood has proven true for my family in my adult years as well. When you move often, you begin to see your community as your family. They are the ones on your emergency call list who know what is driving you crazy at the moment and give you sage advice and a shoulder to cry on. They also become your children's extended family and the ones you celebrate the holiday and special occasions with. Living far away from biological relatives, friends become family—a "framily," if you will. I am so grateful for my football family and my framily. My greatest wish growing up was to be part of a community of loving, fun people. Football and framily have made my dreams come true.

Genuine, authentic friends have been the key to happiness in my life. I don't choose friends based on how many accolades they have or what they can do for me. Todd and I both want a lifestyle in which we have people around us whom we genuinely love and who love us.

True friends don't have an agenda. They're not interested in keeping you small in order to make themselves feel more significant. They want to see you succeed. If you surround yourself with friends, family, and communities who encourage you to reach your full potential, nurture your talents, and affirm your values, you can only move forward. Be grateful and thank God for those friends who elevate and celebrate you. And show that gratitude by becoming the same sort of friend in return. These selfless and generous friends are worth their weight in gold. We are so grateful to have friends who not only love us and make us better people but also adore our kids and are always watching over them.

These special friends have been important to me my whole life. I was blessed with my best friend Sheri in fifth grade, and when we moved, I was afraid I would never have another. She is the closest I have had to a sister. I was lucky to have good friends. I was so unaware of who I was that it was difficult to be a great friend. But over the years, I had the best of girlfriends: roommates, Amy Nell, Sara, Cynthia, Ann, coaches' wives, and colleagues who gave me incredible support, love, and laughter. Although I did not lose all those friends, with the nature of coaching, I learned I was going to have to build a community that was not reliant on my job or Todd's job. So, I created our framily. Just like a family, a framily is full of all kinds of characters, but you get to pick them! Over the years, I have learned that the best framilies need different types of people. No small task, but I seem to be pretty good at picking the right people.

Diversity has played such a critical role in the development of our framily and our football teams over the years. From the Blue Ridge Mountains of West Virginia to south Tulsa, and from the inner loop in Houston to south Pittsburgh and north Scottsdale, we have had the great privilege of sharing our lives with a long list of people from all over the country. In order to have success on the football field, your team must have diverse talents. The quarterback and the defensive tackle certainly have different skill sets, but both can win or lose football games for your team. So, it is a coach's job to identify, recruit, and then develop these diversities into a complete football team. The process is similar for building a diverse and championship-caliber life. Your framily should be made up of a diverse group of people who bring different abilities, skills, and backgrounds to the table to build the fullest life that challenges you to grow.

We live in Scottsdale, Arizona. Our neighborhood and Phoenix are a jumble of people from all over the world. We are surrounded by a wide variety of people. In Texas, we lived around people who were the same as us. I now appreciate the gift of living around people from different parts of the world. We get to enjoy so many different points of view, and we're better people because of it.

Expand Your World

1. **Explore** the world outside your bubble.
2. **Take** up a new hobby.
3. **Go** to new cultural events.
4. **Join** a Bible study or book study group.

This statement from Mike Case illustrates the importance of personal relationships to success: *"Todd and Penni both treated those players like they were their own. I believe that is the reason they were so successful and had great relationships with their players. He was good at making you feel like you were a part of a family, The Tulsa Family."*

Tribe of Gypsies

Coaches' wives laugh when we are characterized as trophy wives. Coaches' wives are the toughest and strongest women I know. Their husbands work long hours, missing family events and holidays. Coaches' wives are left to create a life and take over as CEOs of their families.

The blessing of being a coach's wife is that we pull together. Most of our families are somewhere else, so we become our own family, sometimes traveling from job to job like gypsies. Bowl games become our Christmas celebrations, and spring games are Easter family times. As a coach's wife, it is difficult to know what the future will bring. It is easy to think we can do something about it.

Superhero Coaches' Wives

God makes coaches' wives with superhuman strength. Coaches' wives can move faster than The Flash, lift heads and hearts with more power than Superman, be multiple places more quickly than Nightcrawler, and carry the weight of the world like Atlas.

During spring break and summer, we would often vacation together. We skied in Breckenridge and went to Italy and Mexico. Our kids went to school, played sports, and celebrated birthdays and holidays together. Coaches' wives have many gifts, including knowing how to feed large boys. The first time I had a team meal, one young man, Angel Estrada, ate eleven steaks. I did not serve steaks the next time. My favorite memories are the excitement we shared as a family after big wins! We would sit in the office reliving the explosive plays during the games, taking football family pictures, and calculating what we needed to get to the championship.

One part of the job we dreaded was the months of November and December, which is a time that the rest of the world enjoys. We feared those months because the coaching carousel started then. Would we be moving? How would we decide? Would our friends be moving? Would our friends be fired? How would we deal with our families' stress? Would our kids finish school year or move to join new team? How do you say goodbye? And on and on. Each year, the pressure would build, and each year it seemed to start earlier. We were so happy for those who got opportunities to move up the ladder of success. But when they would leave, it was really like losing family, hard on the heart. For those two months, I always kept my eye on ESPN's Bottom Line, the sports information ticker that crawls across the bottom of the screen. At any time, it could tell us our lives were about to shift.

One of the constants for coaching families is adapting. It is one of the most important skills to thrive as a coaching family.

 **Adaption Actions**

1. **Get** to know your surroundings and identify how they have changed.
2. **Reach** out and initiate the types of relationships that can help you transition and flourish in your new culture.
3. **Use** past experiences to become more efficient at adapting to major changes in your life.
4. **Accept** the challenges that present themselves—mentally, physically, and emotionally.
5. **Embrace** change as adventure and learning opportunities.

This statement by Nick Graham shows the importance of adaptation in the life of a coaching family: "The biggest challenge I face is making sure my wife has an identity of her own. I don't want her to be just 'Coach Graham's wife.' She needs to be **'Candice Graham the business woman.'** Her life doesn't have to revolve completely around me. Coaches' lives are hectic, but the wives that support them [lead] lives [that] are far more hectic. I try my best to provide her alone time and to help her around the house and with the kids."

Engaging Coaches of Character

When Todd hired coaches, he was also inviting people into our football family. He wanted to ensure they were men of strong character with strong teaching skills. Coaching college football requires much more than drawing up schemes and calling a play for a winning game. You want to inspire, motivate, and teach the information you think will not only be critical on the field but also in the rest of these young adults' lives. Due to this coaching philosophy, Todd has had ten assistant coaches go on to be head coaches at major D-1 schools. For many of them, Todd gave them their first NCAA college football coaching job.

He always used what he called the "teacher model." He searched for great men first, men of character, ones who genuinely loved the players and had a unique passion that ignited the souls of everyone on the field. He also hired high school coaches, because they were, first and foremost, educators. Most had teaching degrees, so they were equipped with the teaching strategies and skills necessary to individually educate the players. Most people do not realize how much players have to learn and apply daily. We wanted smart players and the best teachers. Intensive research was needed to find people with these characteristics, followed by a detailed interview process, so no one would be hired based on emotion.

Besides these ten who went on to be head coaches, many others went on to become coordinators at other Division 1 schools and great success in other ways. Every single one of them has something in common: every day they are inspired by our Maker. They want to encourage the players, and they want to win football games. I'm very proud of all the coaches Todd has hired and the many men they have been instrumental in molding, including my husband. They do this in many ways, but probably the most important one is leading by example.

 ### The Following Are Traits of People Who Lead by Example

1. **Speaking** victory in the midst of negativity.
2. **Exuding** positive body language and choosing positive words at all times, especially in adversity.
3. **Setting** your own standards higher than what you ask of others.
4. **Being** humble and kind and always giving respect.

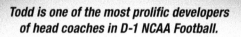

Todd is one of the most prolific developers of head coaches in D-1 NCAA Football.

Our Assistant Coaches: 2006-2017

Chris Ball	Rob Sale
Ron West	Kyle Gray
Keola Loo	Joe Lorig
Chip Long	Trent Figg
Tony Dews	Ray Brown
Herb Hand	Jay Norvell
Jess Loepp	Billy Napier
Todd Dodge	Rob Likens
Bo Graham:	John Simon
David Beaty	Tim Cassidy
Larry Porter	Phil Bennett
Tony Gibson	John Wrenn
Matt Caponi	Tanner Antle
Mike Norvell	Dan Phillips
Jason Jones	Chip Lindsey
Jackie Shipp	Jarred Holley
Dan Lanning	TJ Russian is
Todd Dilbeck	Joe Seumalo
Gus Malzahn	Sam Bennett
Calvin Magee	Graham Craig
Blair Philbrick	Donnie Yantis
Del Alexander	Michael Slater
Rudy Burgess	Matt Bergeron
Danny Phillips	Shawn Slocum
Travis Pelletier	Aaron Pflugrad
Dean Jackson	Marcus Castro
Paul Randolph	Markus Alleyne
Bill Bankenship	Matt Butterfield
Keith Patterson	Brennan Marion
Randall McCray	Sherman Morris
Trevor Dieleman	Kenny Dillingham
Yancy McKnight	Dave Christensen
Shawn Griswold	Andrew Seumalo
Spencer Leftwich	Sammy Lawanson

Our Players Who Became Football Coaches

GJ Kinne	Nick Kelly
Bo Abbott	Brian Pratt
Travis Wike	Taylor Kelly
Carlos Lynn	Kenny Sims
Brad Odom	Jeff Waters
Tanne Antle	Luke Snider
Walter Boyd	Kody Cooke
Josh Newby	Jon Cockroft
Kent Bettley	Jarrod Holley
Willie Carter	Jarrod Holley
Todd Waters	James Casey
Nick Bunting	Adam Federle
Steve Craver	Trey Anderson
Bobby Klinck	Mike Bercovici
Nick Graham	Clint Anderson
AJ Whitmore	Fred Gammage
Cory Bennett	Clint Roundtree
Charles Davis	Grant Martinez
Angel Estrada	Laiu Moeakiola
David Beninati	Drew Mehringer
David Johnson	Nick Henderson
Shannon Carter	Lloyd Carrington
Brennan Marion	Brandon Stewart
Brandon Villareal	John Thompson
Rashad Robinson	Derek Warehime
Jermaine Thaxton	Rod Washington
Frank Ogas III	

Assistant Coaches Who Became D-1 NCAA Head Coaches

Gus Malzahn	Major Applewhite
Chad Morris	Billy Napier
David Beaty	Chris Ball
Mike Norvell	Chip Lindsey
Jay Norvell	Bill Blankenship

GO FROM FRUITLESS TO FORMIDABLE

MIRACLE: MAKING MIRACULOUS CONNECTIONS

Our Tribal Nation: Our Friends and Our Fans!

We have always made an effort to let fans of Todd's teams know they are appreciated. He is so grateful for the support they give. One of my favorite parts of the game is when we become the twelfth man.

It is fourth and 1. The other team decides to go for it. All the fans rise. It is so loud that the other team cannot call a play. They get penalized. The deafening roar continues. The other team starts to hike the ball but becomes disorganized. The linebackers and defensive ends wrap up the quarterback and we get the ball on their 35-yard line. The next play, we throw the ball into the end zone for a touchdown. Now, we own the game— thanks to the twelfth man.

These are the moments when you are no longer an individual. You are part of the team on and off the field. The unity and joy of these times are why football is so popular.

"A day I will never forget is when Penni Graham found me at Devil Walk! We had been communicating on social media for some time beforehand, and I remember hearing, 'Hey baby girl!' I love this woman beyond words. She and Coach Graham entered my life when I felt as if all hope was gone. I truly feel as if knowing them has lifted me up on occasions when I felt I couldn't go on. Which is so out of character for me. Mere words cannot express the love and admiration I have for both Penni and Coach Graham."
—Melissa Cohen

Fans over the years have become more than game day peeps. Our fans have become friends, Frans. Their loyalty and commitment to the team, support for our staff, and our common passion for the success of the team have been the foundation for relationships that have lasted decades. Fans demonstrate some the greatest character traits: loyalty, honesty, forgiveness, generosity, perseverance, optimism, and reliability! (See photos of a few of our best fans in the epilogue.)

The positive energy and joy we experienced from connecting with fans gave us a sense of belonging beyond being the coach and his wife. We were part of the culture, not just the show. Connections like that are so important, but connecting with others can be hard for some, especially the first time.

These Are Some of the Ways You Can Start to Make New Connections

1. **Be genuine** and open. Reach your hand out first.
2. **Destroy barriers.** Make eye contact. If the person is comfortable with it, offer a pat on the back or even a hug.
3. **Be interested.** Ask open-ended questions and listen attentively.
4. **Give a sincere goodbye.** Thank them for their time and tell them that you're glad to have met them or that you hope to talk to them again soon.

These words from Austin Sievert show the importance of establishing connections and the benefits that flow from them:

After ASU clinched the Pac-12 South Division Championship with a 38–33 road win over UCLA, I realized that the team deserved a warm welcome home. I urged Sun Devil fans to meet outside Sun Devil Stadium near the Victory Bell. The goal was to generate a large turnout of ASU fans to greet the Devils upon their arrival from Pasadena. Around 12:30 a.m. on November 24th, 2013, a police escort brought the team back. The Sun Devil faithful descended toward the buses, as "ASU" chants filled the air. Head Coach Todd Graham emerged from the bus, raised his arm in the air, and earned a loud ovation from the crowd. Coach Graham embraced the spirited gathering, thanking each and every fan for staying up late to celebrate. Arizona State players formed a long line, as they shared high-fives, photos, and autographs with their loyal fans. It was moments like these which made the Coach Graham era so special in Tempe. He always made the extra effort to provide accessibility to alumni and fans alike. Coach Graham embraced our traditions, respected our history, and instilled discipline along the way. Restoring Camp Tonto-zona as the preseason training site meant so much to longtime supporters. Coming from a family where my grandfather (Danny Seivert) and father (Dr. Mike Seivert) each played football for Arizona State, the feeling of family was important during Coach Graham's tenure. His positive interactions brought back countless Sun Devil Football alums into the program, which is one of his most underrated accomplishments. The genuine relationship he built with Coach Kush provided a full-circle moment for many Sun Devils. The reputation of the football team improved instantly upon his arrival, thanks to the implementation of the dress code. The sight of ASU players wearing sport coats and dress pants on game day made for an impressive appearance. We will always cherish the fun times shared and special memories created during Coach Graham's time at ASU.

Hanging with Chiefs: Life with the Rich and Famous

I'm not just a coach's wife. I am also a fan. Through football, I have experienced many unbelievable games and met many celebrities. As in most homes in Texas, no matter the economic status, football was king in both of our homes. The Dallas Cowboys ruled the world, and Coach Tom Landry was considered as close to God as a person could get.

Through college football, I have met many former Cowboys coaches and players. They have become friends over the years. I loved getting to know Danny White, Bob Breunig, Darren Woodson, and Dave Wannstedt. I welled up with tears when I met Drew Pearson and Tony Dorsett—totally embarrassing my husband.

In our first bowl game, we played Chan Gailey's Georgia Tech team. Chan Gailey was a former Dallas Cowboys head coach. Todd thought it was weird to ask for a picture with the opposing team's head coach.

At my first College Football Hall of Fame dinner, I was in the elevator with Troy Aikman, Emmitt Smith, Jimmy Johnson, and Jerry Jones. It took everything I had to not squeal! I didn't say a word. I was afraid I might cry if I opened my mouth. However, if anyone else had been in the elevator, I would have a picture. I just carry the picture in my mind.

I met one of my favorite non-Cowboys football players in an elevator at Todd's first game as the Pittsburgh Panthers head coach. I greeted him and introduced myself, my kids, and my helper, Stephanie, who looked like she was going to start jumping up and down. He introduced his friends and then held out his hand and said, "I am Larry (Larry Fitzgerald)." As if we didn't know. I was lucky to sit with him at many events. He was always just as he was on the elevator, so authentic and humble.

I have had the honor of meeting so many people for whom I have incredible admiration. Whether it was at football fundraisers, concerts, or philanthropic events, it was always a gift. However, meeting people at football games was so stressful that my brain couldn't focus. I often felt a bit irritable because I was usually trying to watch the game or talk to a recruit. At games, recruits were more important than any superstar. Luckily, I could usually pull it together to make eye contact, smile, and give a hug. Hopefully I would get a picture, so I could remember things later. There is an endless number of people who have met me on game day whom I cannot recall. I felt like an idiot when I met people for the second or third time. Through my travels I have learned that in many other countries, the phrases "nice to meet you" and "nice to see you" are the same. It would be really helpful in these circumstances.

It is a joy to hear from someone I admire how much they love my husband, but he is rarely present to receive those compliments himself. In fact, unless it is someone or something Todd loves, he avoids public events such as concerts and professional games altogether. If he is there, I spend most of my time at such events taking pictures of him with people who admire him. Even though he appreciates and enjoys people, with social media you never know what might end up on Twitter, so he usually just chooses not to go.

After meeting people and being speechless, or even worse, in tears, I have developed strategies for keeping my cool and making the most of meeting new and exciting people. I keep in mind everyone greets differently. I am comfortable with hugs. I always hug, and I follow up by saying I am from Texas and that is just what we do. As a result, I have gotten to hug a ton of people who are beautiful inside and out.

At most events, there are big and noisy crowds, creating many distractions, so I make sure I have a couple of questions and compliments ready. If I know I will be meeting a specific person, I do a little research in advance, but so often I find myself speaking to someone I never thought I would meet. Here are a few tips you can use for meeting celebrities—even ones you don't know anything about!

Compliments

Everyone loves compliments, and celebrities are used to receiving them. It's a great way to show warmth and appreciation, which is endearing.

 **Meet and Greet Tips:**

Compliments people love:

You make people smile.
You are so special.
You make the world better.
You are such a positive influence.

Asking people questions is the best way to fire up a conversation. This can be difficult if you don't really know what to ask. Here are some questions you can ask anyone:

Sample Questions:

I admire you so much, who do you admire?
What is the scariest part of what you do?
If you weren't a "xxxxxxx," what would you be?
What is your favorite habit?

Jael Mary

In 2014, we were going into the fifth game of the season against USC. Earlier in the season, we had lost our star quarterback, Taylor Kelly, when he broke his foot during a game against Colorado State University. The injury kept him from playing in some of the most treacherous games of the season.

Mike Bercovici stepped up. He had been waiting for the opportunity as Taylor's backup. It was thought that Bercovici might transfer, as he had lost the starting position to Kelly three years earlier. But he stayed, which is evidence that our values of character, smarts, and discipline had made an impact on him. His results had been inconsistent in the games leading up to this one against USC. He had led the win against Stanford but lost the disastrous game at UCLA by having seven or eight turnovers, with many interceptions for touchdowns. It was heartbreaking and hard on Mike. The game with USC was now a must-win situation. Both teams came in with a 3–1 record in conference play. ASU had not won at the Coliseum since 1999. The USC team was very talented, maybe the most talented team the school had seen in the six years Todd had been at ASU.

We were the underdog, and no one had picked us to win. In the first quarter, our defense was effective, only letting seven points make it onto the board. We got the offense moving in the second, and at halftime, the score was 17–15, USC. With both teams making adjustments at halftime, the only points in the third quarter were a field goal for each team. You could hear the discipline and focus on the sideline. Bercovici and Kelly said, with conviction, "We will win this game." They were repeating the sideline slogans: Character. Smart. Discipline. Tough. Together!

Bercovici had over 500 passing yards and four or five touchdowns. He was complemented by Jaelen Strong who had 200 receiving yards and three touchdowns. Our guys were playing lights out. These guys had been to the championship the year before and were a part of our family. They had bought into our values, and together we had a unique identity. All of this was necessary for what was to come at the end of the game.

In the fourth quarter, we had a failed onside kick, and USC pulled ahead by two touchdowns with time running down. We regained possession and threw an out cut to Cameron Smith, who ran over seventy yards to make it a one-score game. We tried another onside kick, but it failed.

Michael Bercovici

Our defense rose to the occasion, forcing USC to go three and out. We had the ball, but with only forty seconds left and no timeouts. Our starting kicker had not made the trip, so we were not confident about trying to kick a field goal. Taking the field, we knew we would have to score a touchdown. I was in the end zone, ready for the picture. I believed in our team. The march down the field included some of the most unbelievable throws and catches in the history of Arizona State, setting up what would be the most critical play in ASU history: the "Hail Mary" to Jaelen Strong, now known as the Jael Mary. With seven seconds left, Mike ("Berco" is what fans called him) dropped back, moving to the right and causing confusion on USC's side of the ball. He threw the ball, and Jaelen tracked it. It was like slow motion, and everybody in the stadium knew what was about to happen. Jaelen knifed in, went up for the ball, and came back down with it in his hands. We were victorious at the Coliseum, with our backup quarterback, on the last play of the game.

The entire game spoke volumes about our values and the goals of our program. There was heart and character in our training and love between our players, and it came to light in that game. Todd impressed upon the players that in life, you're going to get knocked down and you have got to get back up. You can never give up on those people you love. He told them to remember that day, to remember that play. There was nothing that was lucky about it. They had done the work, in practice and in the game. They got themselves into a position to win and followed through. It was their Miracle at the Coliseum.

Jaelen Strong, Man of Character

This story from Janice Hansen illustrates the depth of character Jaelen Strong exhibits, the kind of character we try to develop in all members of our football family:

> One special memory I have of players was at a pregame pep rally at ASU. My daughter, Amy, has a rare disease that makes her bones break easily. She was recovering from a broken femur and had her walker folded near her seat in the stands. At the pep rally, players each had a small football they had autographed that they would throw into the stands. Jaelen Strong was the biggest name on the field, and everyone wanted to catch his football. Much to our surprise, instead of tossing his ball out into the stands, Jaelen walked over to our row. Several fans were reaching out to him, calling his name, trying to snag his attention. It would be heady stuff for a young man. But it didn't turn his head. As he got to the end of our row, he leaned over a couple of people and handed his signed ball to our daughter. It made her night! The fact that he noticed her and went out of his way to make her feel special said a lot about Jaelen Strong, and about the way he had been coached.

Amy Hansen and Penni

TENACIOUS CHARACTER SUMMARY

Serve: Sacrifice for others.

Give: Have a generous spirit.

Acknowledge: Have an "attitude of gratitude."

Listen: Earn respect by showing it.

Celebrate: Appreciate your uniqueness and the diversity of others.

Live it out: Have the courage to lead by example.

Share: Demonstrate genuine authenticity.

Feel: Have empathy for others.

Focus: Concentrate on the little things that make big things happen.

Honor: Act with full integrity, even when no one is watching.

Have Fun! Laugh and enjoy the journey.

ARE YOU A 7 C's SUPERHERO?

Give an example how you have exhibited each action in your life.

Committed. You know when you are committed—you want to achieve your goal, you sacrifice to do it, and your actions support your goal.
Example of Commitment:

Commanding. You know when you have a command over your life—your life isn't fear driven, you do not make excuses, and you do not try to be a people pleaser.
Example of Commanding:

❤ **Compassionate.** You know when you are compassionate—you have a desire to helps others, you are honest and open, you are self-revealing and identify with the struggles of others, and you are grateful for and present in your relationships.
Example of Compassion:

⟲ **Connected.** You know when you are connected—you have trusting and supportive relationships, you behave with respect and kindness, and you have open, meaningful conversations.
Example of Connectedness:

👁 **Captivating.** You know when you are captivating—you bring energy and passion to a room or meeting, you exude charm, and you have a great sense of humor and history.
Example of Captivating:

✻ **Courageous.** You know when you are courageous—you take emotional, financial, mental, or physical risks for positive change your life or the world; you are resilient and preserve through misfortune, affliction and disaster; and you act with dignity and faith, seeking to understand both of yourself and others.
Example of Courage:

⦿ **Creative.** You know when you are creative—you enjoy discovering original ideas, you enjoy finding new solutions and different ways to be more productive, and you can be an open-minded, analytical decision-maker, designer, or speaker when you communicate your creativity.
Example of Creativity:

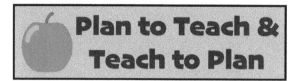

Plan to Teach & Teach to Plan

COMMUNICATE
DAILY

FOCUS ON
INNOVATION
AND
CREATIVIY

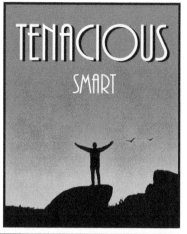

TENACIOUS
SMART

PLAYBOOK

The GRAHAM Game Plan

Opposition's Smart Strategy

The Smart Call Sheet: 7 C's

2
Playbook for
TENACIOUS
SMART

Go from Foolish to Foresight

*"One can never consent to creep when
one feels an impulse to soar."*

—Helen Keller[1]

IT'S A WONDERFUL LIFE

George Bailey lives a life of sacrifice, hard work, and commitment in Frank Capra's classic movie, *It's a Wonderful Life*. Although he doubts his choices, he remains resilient through much adversity. His good deeds cost him what he believed would bring him happiness: going to college and traveling the world. In a moment of despair an angel, Clarence, helps him see how his choices affected so many others and what a disaster his world would have been without George and his hard work, sacrifices, positive attitude, and ability to adapt in the most difficult of circumstances. George Bailey shows us how being smart can save a community and build "a wonderful life!"

---

[1] Address to the American Association to Promote the Teaching of Speech to the Deaf at Mt. Airy, Philadelphia, Pennsylvania (July 8, 1896)

THE GRAHAM GAME PLAN FOR BECOMING TENACIOUSLY SMART

GOAL: Become a Smart Visionary.

RELATIONSHIP: Live *your* purpose.

AGENCY: Move on.

HABITS: Appreciate and apply your abilities.

ADVENTURE: Create a culture of innovation.

MIRACLE: Let education lift you.

OPPOSITION'S SMART STRATEGY

Build a Foolish Mindset in You.

These are the traits that build the foolish mindset:

Abandon your dreams out of cowardice.

Build psychology inflexibility to keep you stuck in the memories past and worries of the future.

Keep your behaviors inconsistent, making you appear fickle.

Believe that you do not have control over your life.

Grow negativity in your expectations.

Isolate yourself from healthy people.

Make excuses to yourself about your bad habits.

Disregard your purpose in life.

Hold on to all regrets.

Maintain a victim mentality.

Use words that pull yourself and others down.

Think you cannot help others.

THE 7 C'S SMART CALL SHEET: TAKE ACTION

1. Be Compassionate.
Move on!
Understand your abilities as a leader.
Appreciate others' abilities.

2. Be Captivating.
Speak victory.
Be elite.
Perform like a dream maker.

3. Be Commanding.
Bring light to your purpose.
Use education to lift you.
Work like an underdog.

4. Be Committed.
Practice habits of tenacity.
Make sacrifices.

5. Be Connected.
Find and apply your abilities.

6. Be Courageous.
Be a victor.
Be a playmaker.

7. Be Creative.
Build a culture of innovation.

GOAL: BECOME A SMART VISIONARY

When you are smart and visionary, a whole new world is opened up to you. You can give purpose to your actions and the actions of people around you, whether those people are your children, your students, your employees, or your teammates in a sport. You develop the ability to solve problems because you can induce and deduce in any environment in order to figure out what needs to be done and who needs to do it.

Being smart helps us receive information from the environment around us and interpret it appropriately, and being visionary helps us provide creative solutions. **Living smart helps us adapt quickly to a rapidly changing environment.** We need to let go of what we think "should" happen in order to learn from the environment what is actually happening. This helps us to adapt and stay innovative as we develop new solutions to old problems. We are always taking in new information and interpreting it in better ways.

The ability to hold on to a ball and make a touchdown for your team is a great metaphor for life, from early childhood to retirement. A football player who can hold on to the ball in any environment—rain, sleet, snow, hail—and can hold on to the ball regardless of being tackled by gigantic players from the opposing team is valuable to his team. For most of us, education is the first thing we learn to hold on to, because it is our first experience outside of the family. I was given the wonderful choice early in my life to hold onto education or take a job. I am grateful that I chose to hold on to the pursuit of education.

Getting a college degree from where I started in life was a tenacious journey that constituted my first leap, the foundation that made almost everything else in my life possible. I did not have a traditional family, but neither did Todd. I was not initially on the college track, but neither was Todd. Despite coming from home environments with limited ambition, we learned to hold on to education as a stabilizing force in our lives. We could not have held on without the tenacity and resilience we learned and the support of our teammates. We were blessed with a great team that coached us including our families, critical teachers and coaches, and stellar teammates, who helped us reach for the stars.

Being wise will not make your dreams come true. To be extraordinary, you must prepare for the future, let go of the present, and embrace change. By becoming a smart visionary, you act before it is completely apparent that you need to do so. For most people, this is difficult. It is what makes great leaders and outstanding players. As Wayne Gretzky shared regarding his success, "I skate to where the puck is going to be, not where it has been." You have to move fast enough to reach your best future. The comfort of the present can seduce you. You have to be willing to sacrifice comfort, resources, and current welfare in the short term for the chaos and risks and uncertainty to create your or your organization's best future. A smart visionary has the capacity to move beyond wisdom to embrace a new and better world.

Penni's Childhood Best Friend

This story from Sheri, my best friend in childhood, illustrates the importance of developing tenacity as early as possible.

> Penni lived with my family for about a year when we were kids. We lived as sisters, sharing a room and all that comes with that. While we are very different, our core beliefs are the same: family, friends, and faith inform our decisions. Back then, Penni had a "sprinter" personality, and I was a "distance runner" type. Her family was different than mine, and I think she sometimes found refuge at our house. It was just more stable (for lack of a better word). When we were in sixth grade, Penni won tickets to the world premiere

of *Grease* on a radio show. We were so excited. We were trying to get permission and a ride to the event when her dad dropped a bomb. He said, "You cannot go until you mow the lawn."

I had a brother who mowed our lawn, so I did not believe that Penni could mow the lawn quickly enough to make it to the premiere. To this day, I have not seen anyone mow a lawn faster than Penni did that afternoon. There was no way that Penni was going to let a little yard work stop her. Thanks to Penni's tenacity, we made it to the premiere.

Tackle with Tenacity

There was a lot of turmoil in my house while I was in high school, so going to college was not on the top of my mind. My mom and adopted dad were going through a disastrous divorce. My mom moved out after she realized she needed help for her alcoholism and could not take care of us. She is now celebrating almost forty years of sobriety. At a young age, I took on many roles in addition to going to school: being a caretaker to my little brother, working at multiple restaurants, participating on the drill team, and taking care of myself. **Because my life was so overwhelming, I doubted my character, intelligence, and capacity. I felt like I did more wrong than right most weeks, a servant of disasters.** I found myself torn about my future and asked myself a lot of questions, such as "Am I good enough for college?" Ultimately, I realized that I had a deep longing in my heart to go to college and earn a degree.

I worked my way through college and paid for it with Pell grants, loans, and help from my parents (when they could manage it). I almost gave up twice: once to become a flight attendant and another time to become a manager for Dave & Buster's. It was the only and original Dave and Buster's. I was tempted both times to take the job and quit school. College felt like an impossible task, but my tenacious spirit would not let me give up. This commitment would be the first of many that did not come easily but built a life that most long for.

It is these choices in life the determine its quality. **It is choices to work a little longer, to think a little smarter, and be a risk taker that keep us on the road to greatness. Our path determines our destination.**

I wonder if I would have the same tenacity today. With Siri, Amazon, and Alexa, I feel like I can wave a magic wand and have almost anything instantly. The media portray stories of "overnight successes" that were decades in the making. The idea of an "instant" environment can create the illusion that there is no need for tenacity. Persistence and perseverance will not get you to your dreams, but they are essential: you won't get to your goals without them. The idea of an "instant" environment can create an illusion that there is no need for tenacity and toughness.

Early in our lives, our parents did not allow us to quit. Today, I do not think that philosophy is prevalent. It seems that if something is "too hard," parents often encourage children to stop. I am so grateful for the gifts of tenacity and toughness that led to my ability to see beyond the present.

 ## Habits of Tenacity

Perseverance: In order to achieve worthy goals, we will go through tough times and have difficult emotions. We must be able to push through and work toward our goals, despite these obstacles.

Adaptability: We must always have or be ready to formulate alternate plans for achievement, because failure is a chance to do things in a new way, not a reason to quit.

Curiosity: It is always helpful to ask others for input and ideas. It's easy to think we know it all, but listening to others can give us the spark we need to ignite our vision.

Super Hero of Tenacity: The greatest example of tenacity that I know of is Helen Keller. Overcoming the adversity of being blind and deaf, Helen Keller was an underdog who became a great teacher, humanitarian, and journalist. She lived eighty-eight years. Although she died in 1968, she is still an inspiration to many. I often look to her wisdom in beautiful quotes like this one: "Character cannot be developed in ease and quiet. Only through experience of trial and suffering can the soul be strengthened, ambition inspired, and success achieved."[2] From her life, I learned that all of us go through tough times and have difficult emotions, but this is part of the process of achieving any worthy goal.

---

[2] Keller, Helen Adams, Helen Keller's Journal: 1936-1937, Doubleday, Doran & company, inc., 1938

RELATIONSHIP: LIVE YOUR PURPOSE

Even though I stayed in college, I was an aimless college student. I would register for school each semester and take six classes but complete only three or four of them because I was busy working. I was so busy working that I sometimes neglected to drop a class, producing a failing grade. I managed to accumulate 130 hours and achieve a C average, but this did not translate into a college degree. On January 25, 1990, I experienced immense joy as my daughter Natalie was born. On that day I discovered a new sense of purpose, and this changed everything. Giving birth gave me a new sense of responsibility as I realized that I could no longer live with uncertainty. My new daughter motivated me to become my best self.

Much of my life, I spent tiptoeing between foolishness and fortitude. Sometimes, I was a genius and other times an idiot. I am so action oriented I did not lack the courage to change before the whole picture was complete, but now it felt my decisions had moral and ethical implications beyond myself. Every day in organizations and homes, we are making decisions that require us do more than what is easy. As leaders, we are required to have the courage to do what is right. **Decisions become tougher when your picture becomes bigger.** It is critical for leaders to understand moral and ethical implications when making choices about the future that impact more than themselves. With the rate of change leaders face today, this is increasingly more difficult.

Like a football player facing a formidable team, I faced seemingly insurmountable odds as a new mother. In 1990, maternity leave lasted only one week and was unpaid. Like many young mothers, I had no health insurance. It is expensive to have a baby, so I worked two jobs to pay the bills that accumulated quickly. It was too hard for me to make the hour-long drive to attend North Texas State University, so I decided to transfer to the University of Texas at Dallas, which was much closer to me. However, I learned from the admissions officers that my 2.4 GPA from North Texas State University made it impossible for me to transfer. Before I became a

> ## "The purpose of life is a life of purpose."

mother, I would have given up if I had faced such an initial obstacle to completing my education.

I didn't give up. The gift of a child in my life created within me a powerful sense of purpose. **Living without purpose is a lot like sailing on an open ocean. The ancient Roman orator Seneca said, "If a man does not know to what port he is steering, no wind is favorable to him."**[3] Purpose is the anchor that keeps us from getting lost in the ocean of life. It keeps you on your course and points you toward the fulfillment of your heart's desire. My new sense of purpose gave me the ability to persevere, despite these new obstacles, and the inspiration to find other paths to achieve the same goal.

I decided to go around the admissions advisers. So, one day in 1990, I spent ten hours at the University of Texas at Dallas. I went to five different departments to plead for admission. At the last two departments, I wore my heart on my sleeve: I cried from fear, exhaustion and frustration. I told the department chairs that I was not leaving until they let me in. My tears produced sympathy and, more important, admission.

With this goal achieved, I faced the next challenge: as a transfer student I first needed to pass college algebra. I had not been in a math class in eight years. To overcome this challenge, I attended community college from 7:00 a.m. to 11:00 a.m. for four weeks, Monday through Friday. I had to attend with my baby daughter, who kept me up at nights, and then went to work after class. This was the first time in my life I was happy to get a "C" in a class.

As Robert Byrne notes, "The purpose of life is a life of purpose."[4]

The gift of a sense of purpose is the gift that keeps on giving. After getting accepted into the University of Texas at Dallas despite my low GPA and after passing college algebra, I was on a roll. My sense of purpose gave me passion, which provided fuel to succeed

---

[3] Seneca, *Epistolae, LXXI.*, 3. Translated from Latin and quoted in Harbottle, Thomas Benfield, *Dictionary of Quotations (Classical)*. London: Swan Sonnenschein & Co., Limited, New York: The MacMillan Co., Limited, 1906

[4] Byrne, Robert. *1,911 Best Things Anybody Ever Said*, New York: Fawcett Books, 1988

as a transfer student. The contrast between this new life and my old life was amazing. Until 1990 I had not reflected on the purpose of my life. At best, I tried to avoid disaster by pleasing people. I let other people and circumstances define my purpose and decision making. By becoming a mother, I suddenly found not only a sense of purpose but a new way of seeing my role in the world. I wanted to hold on to my new sense of purpose and improve the world around me. To improve my understanding of the world around me, I pursued a degree in historical philosophy. In only three semesters, from the Fall of 1990 to the Spring of 1992, I accumulated 51 hours of course work and did my student teaching for a semester to earn my bachelor's degree with honors and a 3.7 GPA. **I would not recommend my path, but I do recommend finding your purpose. I stopped living a foolish life and started having foresight. I had the insight to do what was right.** Because I was on a new path, my confidence in intellectual and creative thinking and abilities grew. Becoming a smart visionary opened the whole world to me.

Over the past twenty-nine years, I have renewed my sense of purpose. A couple of years ago I made it a more formal process. I evaluate my life each year. Instead of making resolutions, I set my purpose for the year. Some years it is about me, and sometimes it is about others. Sometimes it is about learning, sometimes about doing, and sometimes it is even about just being. This year is learning and doing. I will serve on a mission trip in another part of the world, write a book that will help and entertain others, and see as many concerts as I can.

 **Light to Your Purpose**

If you want to develop a sense of purpose, here are some questions you can answer for yourself to **bring light to your purpose**:

- For what do you want to be remembered?
- Do you want to change the world? If so, how?
- If you could go anywhere and do anything, what would it be?
- What makes you forget about the rest of the world?
- If you had a year to live, what would you do?
- If you could learn anything, what would it be?

Remember, if you want to live a life with a sense of purpose, do not let your life sway on the seas. Do not let other people define your purpose. Sometimes your purpose will find you: seek discernment from God, friends, and family.

AGENCY: MOVE ON

"Don't let a win get to your head or a loss to your heart."
—Chuck D[5]

This quote applies to any victory and any loss. The fact is, every person loses more games than they win. Every athlete on every team knows that they are not going to win every game. The most important part of a loss is not the physical act of losing the game, but the mental challenge of viewing yourself as either a loser or a winner. If you play the next game by thinking of your loss in the previous game, all the regret and shame inside of your heart will prevent you from playing at your best. The only way athletes can move forward in any sport is by accepting that the last game was merely their last game. The next game is where all the action is, where all their mental and emotional focus must be. The only way to prepare for the next game is to bring positive lessons from the previous games. **There is no room for regret and shame in life as we look forward to the next game.**

As Todd and I both quickly earned our graduate degrees, I stayed focused on my academic and professional career, but Todd's coaching career took a turn suddenly. Before we were married, I had intended to finish my PhD, then become the chief executive officer of a large corporation after five years. However, Todd took a coaching position at West Virginia University (WVU) three months after we were married. It was a shock to our world, because he took pay cut to move from Texas high school football to Division 1 college football. This move required me to leave my six-figure career. To make our situation worse, our kids did not want to leave their family and friends. We bore the cost of flying them regularly to and from Texas

5   Stills, Stephen, Chuck D, and LaQuantum Leap, "He Got Game (Album Version)", Public Enemy, *He Got Game*, Polygram, 1998

to Morgantown, West Virginia. We also had three people living in our basement and teams of visitors.

As Todd's career took off, my career had to be whatever was available, and my heart quickly filled with regret. My desire to get my PhD turned into a big obstacle in our marriage and our family life. I ended up attending ten universities—three to get my undergraduate degree and seven as a post-graduate student. I earned my master's degree while I was a single mom with two kids and working too many hours, before Todd and I married. I started my PhD before we got married. I began writing my dissertation at WVU, but I had to start over again every time Todd moved up the ladder to a new coaching job. I worked on degrees in education leadership, technology education, curriculum and instruction, instructional technology, instructional psychology, educational psychology, and social technology. Every time, I had to start over, my heart filled with regret from not finishing the previous degree. Unfortunately, I had little control over the circumstances. Within six years of our wedding, Todd went from beimg a high school coach to being head football coach at Rice University.

Sadly, I let the frustration and insecurity build up inside of me, sometimes lashing out and getting depressed because I longed for the PhD. My kids nicknamed me "Dr. Mom." So many times when we are frustrated and insecure, we waste so much energy and power on the wrong purpose. When you see your temper rising, become sensitive to what the underlying causes might be. I evaluated my worth as a person by the letters that would follow my name. After much soul-searching, I realized my sense of worth should never be attached to something so worldly as an academic degree. I wanted to inspire people to make a difference in our community and our home. I needed to be driven by a noble passion; this was the cause of my frustration.

As a smart visionary, I could enhance my core values from the long-term desire to earn a PhD to the pursuit of an excellent, everyday life filled with learning. The world will always value growth. My graduate education included a variety of disciplines and fields; as result, the knowledge I acquired has more breadth and depth than if I had stayed in one place and only earned a PhD. By changing my values from acquiring status as a possession to developing wisdom and connection to other people, all my wishes came true. **When we can see beyond short-term desires with eyes that**

are open to all possibilities, our lives are filled with positive and optimistic thoughts and emotions.

Before this realization, I carried regret for over ten years. When I finally let go of this regret and moved on, I was shocked by how light I felt. I have since learned to view all my regrets as learning opportunities. **Regrets** hurt your brain because your brain will hold on to unresolved issues. **Regrets** drain your energy and time. **Regrets** ruin companies because the weight of regret on organizations pulls against positive change. Resolve your regrets, forgive yourself, and *move on*!

If you need to, read a book, find a counselor, or talk to a friend. Sometimes one session with a counselor will help you move on.

> Sometimes we need to take a Demi Lovato attitude:
> "Sorry, I'm not sorry."

You simply do not have a time machine to go back and make a different choice. Even if you could make a different choice, the new choice might cause unintended consequences that you wouldn't like. What we see as mistakes are in fact actions that lead to positive outcomes.

If I have a regret that bubbles up, I ask myself about the people, places, culture, and values I was experiencing during that time. After examining these areas, I can better see why I made that choice, appreciate how I have grown, and move on.

 How to *Move On*

Pondering these questions will help you as you try to move on and move forward:

- What are your regrets?
- What will happen if you see the regret as a learning experience?
- What new insights do you have about yourself since you made the choice?
- Are there any actions you need to take?
- How would you do it differently now?
- How have a grown since that choice?
- What will you happen if you say, "Sorry, Not Sorry"?

Moving on allows us to play big! Let your brain and heart view regrets as an informing experience and the future as a new adventure free from weight of past that you cannot change. Moving on allows us to play big and have a big life!

HABIT: APPRECIATE YOUR ABILITIES

"My life has been pretty much about my family.

My parents were my father and a very dear grandmother. My dad was very strict and taught us to work hard to be successful. Education was important. My grandmother worked hard to take care of her nine children and me and my sister. She always had a song in her heart and loved our Lord and Savior. She taught me to love and to share and to always be kind to others.

I married very young and had five children. I was happy, and I loved being a mother. The most successful people are those who learn to work when they are young and learn the value of education."

—Carol Graham, Todd's mother

There was zero expectation for Todd to go to college. Todd was a successful student. Learning was easy for him. It is hard to believe now, but his seventh-grade teacher, Cheryl Murf, told me how quiet and shy he was in the classroom. He was one of only two in his family to graduate from high school, and the only one to attend college. After high school his dream was to become a Marine, but a single conversation changed his future. Todd's high school football coach, **Gary Childress, taught him that heart and intellect are critical in learning and in life, and that he would have to develop both if he wanted to accomplish his goals.**

Todd found out he was going to become a father during his junior year of high school. Immediately, Todd got a job so that he could financially support the baby. Gary, Todd's high school football coach, went to his mom and said, "Todd is not going to become a statistic. He's going to finish high school. He will go to football practice and he can work at the Shell station in the evenings. He is going to graduate from high school, and he is going to college." If not for Gary, Todd probably would have been just another statistic in a low socioeconomic area. Todd took full advantage of football and graduated from college in three-and-a-half years. Being smart was another trait Todd discovered.

"I remember spending hours breaking down film and giving Coach Graham the report, and he could look over it for twenty minutes and have it all memorized."

—Shannon Carter, current head football coach, former football player for the Tulsa Golden Hurricane, and former professional baseball player

There are two kinds of strengths all humans have: natural abilities and learned skills. Todd was born a natural athlete. At thirty, he could still outrun every one of his athletes and do a standing back flip. Often, we focus on skills we want to acquire but fail to acknowledge and optimize the gifts that we are born with. Abilities are natural gifts, whereas skills can be learned through experience and education. No matter how many degrees I acquire, I could never bench press over 250 pounds as Todd can at age 54, just like I could never be a mascot like Michael.

"Michael grew up in the locker room with the players."
—Vi Teofilo, former Sun Devil, two-time honorable mention All-Pac-12.

Michael was the only child born after Todd became a D-1 football coach. When he was small, he was frustrated and at times frightened by the bands and mascots and fireworks—they are all part of college football gala atmosphere but made game days exponentially stressful for me. One day, though, Michael discovered his ability to be the mascot. When he found his ability, it changed our game days forever. Through Michael's innate personality to engage and entertain people, he was no longer the coach's son; he was part of the team. His ability to be a mascot carried over to the rest of his life. He understood at an early age that making the most of his abilities and passions would be his key to open the doors of his future.

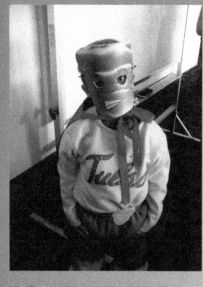

Michael the Mascot

"I have become close with the youngest Graham, Michael, over the years and the thing that always sticks out to me is how driven he is. I don't think I have ever met a teenage boy with the goals, character, and determination that he has. He is all around such a great kid with a big heart, and I know it's because of his parents and their example."

—Margaret Kreyling, close family friend.

Owning our natural abilities is important because our abilities empower us to live life more fully.

Margaret and Michael

It is difficult to see our own natural abilities, so here is a list. Go through the list. Circle the words that seem both natural and describe a trait you have. Put an "x" over those words that least describe you. Go to TheChampsofChange.com to find more activities to identify your abilities.

Find Your Abilities

Creative	Logical	Persistent	Analytical
Hard-working	Problem solver	Ethical	Detail-Oriented
Structured	Intellectual	Innovative	Imaginative
Focused	Visionary	Music	Painting
Writing	Hiking	Jumping	Running
Swimming	Shooting Guns	Concentration	Endurance
Willpower	Farming	Debate	Research
Speak Language	Knowledge	Leadership	Oratory
Awareness	Empathy	Act	Comedian
Dance	Sing	Charm	Interrogate
Persuade	Navigating	Public Speaking	

 **Apply Your Abilities**

By considering the following questions, you will start learning how to apply your abilities.

- How would you describe yourself based on the abilities you have and ones you do not?
- Making the most of your abilities can increase your success in your personal and professional life. How can you optimize your abilities?
- Be aware of others' abilities. Look for other people's abilities and acknowledge we all have different abilities. This can reduce stress, producing creative and innovative results. A common mistake many people make in their professional and personal lives is expecting others to have the same abilities they have. Analyze a friend and coworker's abilities. How can your abilities complement theirs?

It is natural for us to compare our abilities to other people's abilities. We universalize our own abilities and expect other people to have them. Or we universalize other people's abilities and experience shame or regret if we have not developed similar abilities. The important news is that we are all different, so each of us was born with natural abilities.

 ## Understand Abilities as a Leadership

As a leader, it is critical to have compassionate understanding of abilities. We all have shortcomings and limitations. Leaders need a keen judgement to balance the need of individual with organization. **The best leaders help everyone in the organization experience the importance and value of their contribution.** One way for your organization to feel importance and value is by Speaking Victory.

 ## Speaking Victory

Speaking victory is most important in the face of adversity. **Speaking victory** means using your words to lift up rather than pull down, to confess your faith in the victory that lies ahead. But it must include backing up those words with actions—believing in and working towards the plan, never giving up or losing hope because instant gratification is not an option. **Speaking victory** allowed us to be a part of three of the biggest turnarounds in college football. It allowed the West Virginia Mountaineers, who were 3–9 in 2002, to rebound to a 9–3 record in 2003. It propelled the Tulsa football program from one conference win in two years to an 8–4 record and a bowl berth the next year. It allowed the 2006 Rice Owls, who started 0–4, to rebound to 7–6 finish and earn the first bowl berth in forty-six years. **Speaking victory** is how you respond at critical points of adversity along the road in life. Having a plan and thriving in an adverse environment are the keys to turnarounds on the field and in life. **Speaking victory** allows you to lift yourself and others above the surrounding circumstances, whether it be at home, at work, or on the field. Todd used his natural abilities to create opportunities for himself. He also spoke victory constantly over his own life and the lives of others.

Student Athletes—Superheroes of the 7C's

Did you know that right at two-thirds (66 percent) of incoming freshmen will leave college after their first year? Compare that to the fact the NCAA reported that almost nine out of ten student athletes—87 percent—graduated with a bachelor's degree last year. Student athletes were able to achieve this despite the fact they face overwhelming schedules and significantly greater responsibilities than the average college student. How do they do it?

In the case of student athletes I have known, the "7 C's" identify what the special "something" that can distinguish student athletes from general population students and explain the success of student athletes.

Student Athletes exemplify the 7 C's!

Committed. Student athletes give up sleep, social life, and family time to gain what most of their parents never had a chance to achieve: a college degree, an opportunity to excel in the classroom, on the playing field, and—most importantly—earn their piece of the American Dream.

Commanding. Student athletes push themselves to be better. Unlike most of the general student population, student athletes work every day to be better by using all the resources available to them, owning their success on and off the field.

Compassionate. Students athletes seek out opportunities to help others. At a far higher rate than the general student population, student athletes volunteer in the community, helping to bring a smile to those in need. Student athletes also take their time to love the fandom with handshakes, hugs, and pictures.

Connected. Student athletes know part of cultivating a winning team requires positive bonding of its members. Student athletes know that 1+1=3; they give more of themselves than even they originally imagined. A lineman receives help from teammate to complete a block, which results in a pass for a touchdown; in almost every case, a touchdown requires all eleven players on the field communicating and working together toward that goal. Student athletes, probably more than most, understand the importance of connectedness.

Captivating. Student athletes have a tenacious drive and spirit. Student athletes have mental, physical, and emotional abilities that capture our attention on the field and our admiration in the classroom.

Courageous. Student athletes has a tenacious work ethic and dedication in the face of all sorts of adversity. Student athletes are willing to go through the pain and suffering to support their team, overcoming obstacles that others can only imagine.

Creative. Student athletes must to be creative across a variety of disciplines, both on and off the field. Student athletes organize their time and work in unique ways to meet the numerous demands on them. Student athletes use split-second decision making and problem solving on the field. Student athletes look for new and innovative ways enhance physical and mental performance. Student athletes understand that to succeed in life, one must always be better now than they were before—constantly improving mental and physical performance to reach their fullest potential.

Playmakers

We mention many playmakers throughout the book who changed games and seasons. Here are some outstanding playmakers who used their natural abilities and inspiring words to lift themselves and their team to play at the next level.

Charles Clay, fullback, Tulsa

Charles Clay: Charles provided a versatile offensive weapon with size that Todd could line up almost anywhere on the field, from tight end to quarterback in the wildcat formation, for his entire coaching tenure there. Over four years he scored thirty-eight touchdowns, twenty-eight of them receiving. He caught 189 passes and ran the ball 179 times in a Tulsa uniform without ever fumbling. He was chosen by the Miami Dolphins in the sixth round of the 2011 NFL draft, and has gone on to a solid eight-year career as an NFL tight end with the Dolphins and Buffalo Bills, signing with the Arizona Cardinals as a free agent for 2019.

D. J. Foster, running back, Arizona State

D. J. Foster: Todd has always loved players like D. J., who can produce both as a runner and a receiver. He was one of only five NCAA players to amass 2,000 running and 2,000 receiving yards. He made big plays (two touchdowns against Stanford in the 2013 PAC-12 championship) and served where needed, playing primarily as a wide receiver his senior year after rushing for 1,081 yards as a junior. Although he was not chosen in the NFL draft, D. J. won a spot as a free agent on the New England Patriots' 2016 world championship team. He earned more playing time in 2017 after the Atlanta Falcons claimed him from the Patriots' squad and then returned home to the Arizona Cardinals.

Aaron Donald, Pittsburgh: Before establishing himself as one of the NFL's D-line superstars with the Los Angeles Rams, Aaron showed Todd what the future would bring during his sophomore year in 2011. He became a starter that season and lit up the Big East with eleven sacks and forty-seven tackles, including sixteen for a loss. His combination of strength and speed (4.68 40-yard dash, a record for defensive tackles at the NFL combine) earned him virtually every major college defensive award over four years at Pitt, and the Rams snapped him up with the thirteenth pick in round one of the 2014 NFL draft.

Damarious Randall, defensive back, Arizona State

Damarious Randall: Much to Todd's delight, Damarious chose football over baseball, and he made it work. Transferring to ASU from junior college for his junior year in 2013, he racked up seventy-one tackles, three interceptions, and a touchdown after missing his first four games with a leg injury. After a big senior year in which he led the team with 106 tackles, the Green Bay Packers took him with the thirtieth pick in the first round of the 2015 NFL draft. He was traded to the Cleveland Browns in 2018 and has intercepted fourteen passes, returning two for touchdowns, over his first four years in the NFL.

N'Keal Harry, wide receiver, Arizona State

N'Keal Harry: "Insane" was a popular way to describe some of the plays N'Keal made during his three years in Tempe. He was a starter from his first day in uniform, earning several freshman All-America honors and turned it up as a sophomore with eighty-two catches for 1,142 yards. His junior year turned into a highlight reel, with a memorable one-handed catch and punt return touchdown against USC, and nine catches with three touchdowns for 161 yards in a late-season upset of fifteenth-ranked Utah. He then declared for the 2019 NFL draft, and the New England Patriots chose him with the thirty-second and final pick of the first round.

G. J. Kinne, quarterback, Tulsa

G. J. Kinne: A transfer from the University of Texas after being heavily recruited out of high school, G. J. started for three years at Tulsa and threw for 9,472 yards and eighty-one touchdowns. He then earned MVP honors in the 2012 NFLPA Collegiate Bowl. After bouncing around four different pro leagues as a player, he entered the coaching profession in 2017. After stops at SMU and Arkansas, in 2019 he joined the offensive staff of the Philadelphia Eagles, where he had been a member of the team's practice squad in 2014.

"Playing at the University of Tulsa for Coach Graham taught me that anything is possible with hard work. We proved that to be true in 2010 when Tulsa defeated Notre Dame in South Bend. That moment will always stay with me as an accumulation of the power of teamwork, mental and physical toughness, and great leadership."

—G. J. Kinne

Tyler Jack, East Central University: In 1993, Todd's third and final season as defensive coordinator at his alma mater, Tyler helped lead his school to the NAIA Division 1 national championship. Tyler powered the offense, setting a single-game rushing record of 318 yards that still stands at the now-NCAA Division 2 school.

Jarett Dillard, wide receiver, Rice University

Jarett Dillard: In 2006 Todd and the Rice Owls clenched their first bowl berth in forty-five years. During that season Jarett Dillard finished as an ESPN 1st Team All-American, setting many Rice receiving records as well as the NCAA record for consecutive games with at least one touchdown catch (10). Jarett was a Biletnikoff finalist in 2006 and finished his Rice career as the NCAA leader in touchdown receptions (60). Jarett was drafted in the fifth round of the 2009 draft to the Jacksonville Jaguars. He enjoyed a five-year career in the NFL before returning to Texas where he now practices law at Kilpatrick Townsend in Houston.

Will Sutton, defensive line, Arizona State

Will Sutton: In 2012 and 2013 Todd's defense at ASU was one of the most disruptive and exciting defenses in the country. During that time the most dominant defensive football player on the West Coast was Will Sutton, unprecedented two-time PAC-12 Pat Tillman Defensive Player of the Year and All-American. In 2012 alone Will finished with fourteen sacks and fifteen tackles for loss helping the ASU defense dominate in several major NCAA Team Defensive categories. In 2013, the NCAA ranked ASU #2 in the nation in team sacks with Sutton devouring opposition. Will was drafted in the third round of the 2014 draft by the Chicago Bears.

Damaris Johnson, wide receiver and punt returner, Tulsa

Damaris Johnson: Arguably the most exciting offensive football player to watch in all of Todd's career was wide receiver and kick returner Damaris Johnson at the University of Tulsa. Although small in stature, standing only five feet and eight inches and weighing 175 pounds, Damaris was the most explosive and breathtaking offensive skill player we have ever had the pleasure of coaching. In just three seasons at The University of Tulsa, Damaris broke the NCAA record for all-purpose yards in a career as well as becoming the all-time NCAA leader in kick return yardage in a career. He was also one of a long list of freshman All-Americans Todd has coached and received multiple All-Conference selections. Damaris signed as an undrafted free agent with the Philadelphia Eagles in 2012 and also played for the Texans, Patriots, and Titans before finishing in the CFL in 2016.

Jaelen Strong, wide receiver, Arizona State.

Jaelen Strong: Jaelen was one of several impact players who emerged at ASU during our back to back 10-win seasons in 2013 and 2014. He was a headache for many Pac-12 secondaries, dominating the league in both seasons with a combined 157 receptions with a total of 2,287 yards and 17 touchdowns. Jaelen was drafted as the seventieth overall pick in the third round of the NFL draft to the Houston Texans. He would then go on to play with the Jacksonville Jaguars and is now currently signed with the Cleveland Browns

"I think the most memorable moment in my football career was the Hail Mary vs. USC. Simply because I learned much about perseverance in such little time. We had almost no chance to win the game, but we kept fighting and fighting and won the game. I believe to persevere you have to have a certain amount of humility about yourself. You have to know your weaknesses and what you thrive off of. I am blessed to play the game of football because it has taught me many core values of life."

—Jaelen Strong

Underdogs are Game Changers

Everyone can learn from underdogs

In my experience, most underdogs have a strong spiritual faith that inspires and motivates them to relentlessly strive to reach their goals. They are the toughest and most tenacious. **Underdog players illustrate the values we hold dear.** They have character. Their courage and sense of responsibility eliminate their limitations. Their discipline facilitates a work ethic and behaviors that promote them to new levels. Their toughness enables them to withstand adverse conditions and hardships. Their intellect gives them a unique perspective and ability to think differently and develop risk-taking ability. Todd always loved finding the underdogs.

One and Onlys: One Offer to Play D-1 College Football

"One and onlys" are players who received one offer to play for only one team in Division 1 football. Like underdogs, they are usually not born with Olympian abilities. To achieve at the highest levels, they focus on doing what does not require ability but that few are willing to do.

We were the only major college to make an offer for these four players to play Division 1 football.

We were able to identify greatness in these young men that others could not see. There is something about an underdog that makes them fight harder and become winners. The proof is in the careers of some outstanding players we gave a chance by selecting them to Tulsa, and only Tulsa, to play college ball. These players are a testament to the fact that it doesn't matter how many "nos" you get; all that matters is getting the right "yes"! **It just takes one "yes" to make your dreams come true.**

The following four players came to play for Tulsa in the early 2000s, helping them turn around a losing program by giving the Golden Hurricane everything it asked for. The result was a golden era of success in Tulsa football history.

Nelson Coleman

Nelson Coleman: Nelson played only one year of varsity high school football, yet that year was enough to convince Coach Graham he belonged on the college gridiron. Nelson displayed the heart, grit, and intelligence it takes to be an elite champion. During his tenure from 2003–2007, he was not only a smart, hard-hitting linebacker, but a respected leader, recognized by players and coaches, both on and off the field. One of his most memorable plays came in the 2005 Liberty Bowl, when he picked off a pass late in the game, allowing Tulsa to hold on to a 31–24 victory over Fresno State. He turned his one and only offer into an all-conference career and is the leading tackler in Tulsa football history. He now is a very successful businessman in Dallas, Texas.

Chris Chamberlin

Chris Chamberlain: Chris exemplified the core values of our program. He had tremendous faith and character that produced a smart, disciplined, and physically tough player on the field. His intelligence and preparation allowed him to be one of the smartest players we ever coached. Another star in the 2005 Liberty Bowl, Chris Chamberlain racked up eleven tackles as linebacker that day. The nimble, 6'2", 225-pounder consistently ranked high in the conference for solo tackles and assists, earning three letters thanks not only to hard hitting but intelligence. Chris went on to play for the St. Louis Rams, where his nineteen tackles led the Rams' special teams one year. He ended his long professional career with the New Orleans Saints because of injuries. He has moved on to serve his community in Oklahoma City as a firefighter.

"Coach Graham had a huge impact on my football career and life. He totally reset my perspective on effort when my first year on campus he let us know that 'maximum effort was the minimum expectation!' This is a principle I've adopted and shared with others aspiring to be great and reach their full potential."
—Chris Chamberlin

Shannon Carter

Shannon Carter: Safety Shannon Carter began his career at Tulsa full of promise, after a minor league baseball career that spanned six years with Baltimore and Toronto. Helping the Golden Hurricane turn around several losing seasons, in 2003 Shannon proved himself a physical player, tallying up double-digit tackles in several games. His work ethic, discipline, and leadership were elite. A leader on the field, he was touted as the quarterback of our defense. He was one of the best leaders we ever coached in over thirty years. Unfortunately, injuries cut his career short in 2005, after which he went on to take on coaching roles for the Golden Hurricane. He now has a successful career as a high school football coach in Texas and has just recently been selected to his first head-coaching job.

> *"Just the feeling of being so prepared all week that*
> *the game was always easier than practice."*
> —Shannon Carter

Nick Graham #22

Nick Graham: Nick will forever be remembered as the Tulsa player who in 2006 blocked a Navy extra point attempt on the final play to give the Golden Hurricane a 24–23 win. He also had the key interception against Central Florida in 2005 that sealed the first Conference USA (CUSA) championship in Tulsa football history. A three-year letter winner, in 2005 Nick was ranked eighth nationally in interceptions, earning him a spot on the second team All-Conference USA. He went on to play professional ball for Philadelphia (2007) and Indianapolis (2008–2009) as well as in the Canadian Football League (CFL). He has moved on to a successful college coaching career at McNeese State in Louisiana.

Nick Graham describes the rewards that come from sacrifice and hard work: "I just remember calling my mom and crying with her when I made my first NFL roster. All my life I just wanted to make her proud of me. She gave her everything to me and just giving her that piece of happiness meant everything to me."

 **Make Sacrifices**

When you are an underdog, you have to out-work, out-smart and make sacrifices in order to reach goals others might think impossible. Almost all "overachievers" exhibit the skill to **sacrifice in these three ways**.

1. **Delaying gratification.** Resisting the impulse to satisfy immediate desires in favor of greater value in the future creates opportunities only for those willing to wait.

2. **Placing others' needs before their own.** Sacrificing for others builds social connections, improves health, and makes a person happier.

3. **Abandoning bad habits.** Letting go of bad habits may be one of the toughest sacrifices, because we are fighting with the deepest part of our own minds.

Sacrificing is something everyone can do, but it is not an innate ability. It is a tool we can all use to reach our goals and dreams.

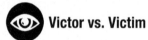 **Victor vs. Victim**

The difference between being a victor and a victim is your mind-set. It is how you train yourself to respond to circumstances that arise throughout life. In even in the most difficult situations, victors find a way to win.

Victors take responsibility, hope, grow, overcome adversity, set high expectations for themselves, feel free, and do hard things.

Victims feel trapped, do what seems easy or habitual, let others control their world, worry, think other people are luckier, and indulge in blame and envy.

Dream Makers

To be a dream maker, you have to be a victor, not a victim.

I have watched the angst and work traditional high school players go through to make it to the next level, only for many of them to have their dreams of college football scholarships shattered. Probably no one values and appreciates the football scholarship more than those players who came up the hard way, facing overwhelming obstacles. Two players who beat the odds and went on to star at Tulsa and Arizona State, respectively, are Brennan Marion and Marion Grice. Nothing was going to stop their dreams from coming true.

Brennan Marion

Brennan Marion: Brennan Marion found it common to be surrounded by violence. His cousin was shot, and when his grandmother passed, he found himself ineligible to play high school football. Determined to play college ball after a standout high school career, in 2005 he joined the football squad at Foothill Community College in Los Altos Hills, California, and then De Anza Junior College outside San Francisco. Making teams and showcasing one's talent is hard enough, but Marion had to do it as a homeless person. It seems he and some other out-of-state teammates spent months sleeping in locker rooms, on buses, and even once in the press box after their living stipend fell through. Brennan told me Skittles served as his main meal.

But his hard work paid off when he received an offer from Tulsa football. Coach Graham recalls meeting with him in his office and seeing the passion and sacrifice in his eyes, showing that he just needed someone to believe in him. Marion was soon setting records as a wide receiver in everything from receptions to yards per catch. He received the last scholarship of 2007. The future looked a whole lot brighter than the past. Then a torn ACL ended his prospects. Though he would eventually sign with the Miami Dolphins, followed by the Montreal Alouettes of the CFL, the recurring ACL problem ended his career.

But it did not end his love of football.

Ever determined, Marion turned to coaching, first high school then college, eventually landing a job as offensive coordinator and quarterbacks' coach at Howard University. When head coach Mike London left for The College of William and Mary at the end of the 2018 season, he made sure he brought his standout offensive coordinator along for a new stint and a future that gets brighter all the time.

These are words that made an impact on Brennan:

You are Victor not a Victim"
—Todd Graham

"Dream Big"
—Gus Malzahn

"To Whom Much is Given Much is Required"
—Brennan's Grandfather

Mike London and Chris Thomsen really taught Brennan what Jeremiah 29:11 means.

Marion Grice

Marion Grice: Marion Grice was highly recruited by the biggest and best universities in the nation. He was a superstar high school athlete at Chester Nimitz High School. He grew up in a tough area in part of Houston, facing adversity most of us cannot imagine. When he was a sophomore, he lost his father. After a prank gone wrong, he was in legal trouble. Grice was forced to go the junior college instead of a university. Instead of having a victim's mentality, Grice went to Blinn Junior College, not far from Houston.

Marion Grice came to ASU rated as the #1 running back in junior college football while playing at Blinn. Grice certainly had a heart as big as Texas but decided to take the trip to Tempe at the last minute. He found his new home, a place far away from Houston where his family was. Because of Grice's unique talent, he could have gone to almost any school in the nation.

Our son Bo had the privilege of coaching him his senior season at ASU. Bo tells us: "Marion [Grice] is one of the smartest players I have ever coached. He knew the offense in and out, and you could tell he grew up playing the game. He was one of the few ball carriers that I have come across that could see the entire field and set up his blocks. Not only a first-class runner, he also had some of the best hands on the team. He was a gamer; when the lights came on, he could take it to another level."

Just days before the team departed for the San Francisco Kraft Bowl Game, his last as Sun Devil, Grice received news from back home that his brother Joshua had been shot and killed in front of their home for a pair of shoes.

In honor of Joshua, Grice responded like a true champion and rushed for 159 yards and two touchdowns and was named the offensive MVP.

He would finish his ASU career (just two seasons) as a Hornung Award finalist and a two-time All-Pac 12 selection and was on the list of possible Heisman nominees. In just twenty-four games he scored 234 points and thirty-nine touchdowns, fifth in ASU history, and was the only player in the NCAA to eclipse 500 yards in all three categories: rushing, receiving, and returning. After suffering an injury his senior season at the Rose Bowl in a hard-fought victory over UCLA, Grice missed the last three games of the year and still finished third in the country in all-purpose yards per game (176.45) and fifth in the country in points scored per game (10.9).

Grice would go on to be drafted in 2014 by the Chargers and would become the first college graduate in his family. A well-traveled pro career took him to four NFL and two CFL teams, the highlight being his touchdown for the Arizona Cardinals in a 20–14 playoff game.

Todd Was an Underdog,

Sheree, Todd's Sister Standing with Sign

This story comes from Sheree, Todd's sister:

My brother Todd is the strongest person I know. He's a self-made man built from the ground up. There's nothing that comes his way that he can't rise up from. Life changes that destroy some drive him. He doesn't know the word "quit." He's the only person that never gave up on me and makes me feel I can do things. He's the best brother a girl could have. I'm proud of my brother's success and grateful for everything he has done for me. Life's struggles made me hard and angry, so I'm not easy. He has taken care of my mom for many years and been a blessing to her and our family. Todd isn't like my dad at all. You can depend on him, and no matter what, he won't abandon you. His success gave me Friday night lights full of priceless memories that will last forever. From Allen High to Tulsa, Rice and ASU, there are so many to remember them all, but a few stand out, like beating Fresno in the AutoZone Liberty Bowl or Jared Dillard catching the winning TD pass on his back in the end-zone to beat SMU. Obviously, I'm his favorite sister!

"Coaches work hard everywhere, but I believe Todd has the ability that wherever he has gone he has outworked them all."
—Bucky Allshouse

HABIT: APPRECIATE YOUR ABILITIES • **97**

Good to Elite: Taylor Kelly

Taylor Kelly and Todd at wedding

Although Taylor Kelly did not face the same hardships, when we arrived at ASU, Taylor was seen as an underdog. I have seen lots of young men come into and out of our lives. So many were exceptional young men, but Taylor Kelly really stands out for his tenacity. He fought to be the absolute best at all he did.

In three years as the starting quarterback for Arizona State University, Taylor led his team to twenty-nine victories. Victories on the field, however, tell only a small part of his story. When my husband arrived at Arizona State, Taylor was a good student, carrying a 3.4 GPA, and he was the third-string quarterback. For Taylor, though, "good enough" was not good enough.

He told my husband he wanted to be the best. Todd said the best was a 4.0 GPA. In three years, he went from good to elite, and was a finalist for the Campbell Award, known as the "Academic Heisman" as it goes to the college football player with the best combination of on-field ability and academic achievement.

Taylor's natural and developed leadership made a difference. Todd says Taylor made him want to be a better coach. He had that same impact in the locker room with his fellow players. He reached out to first-year walk-ons and defensive players. His example constantly inspires others to improve themselves.

Offense, defense, special teams—everyone on the team and on the coaching staff was inspired to be better in the weight room, on the practice field, and when the pressure was on during a big game. He had wins over "blue bloods" like USC, UCLA, Notre Dame, and just about every team in the PAC-12, leading the Sun Devils to the 2013 PAC-12 South Championship, so that ASU hosted the first Pac-12 Championship game ever in the history of Sun Devil football by posting the best record in conference play for 2013 season.

He gave so much of himself; he has a servant's heart. Todd used to always tell Taylor that he wanted him to marry our daughter. For a dad, there is no higher praise he can heap on a young man. As a mom, I could not have agreed more. Of course, we said this only as a testament to Taylor's character, which he now shows as husband to his incredible wife, Erin,

---

Winning as the Underdog

We played some of our more memorable games as underdogs, and they are fan favorites!

2006 Rice vs. Tulsa. Rice, a 17+ underdog, won at Tulsa

2010 Tulsa vs. Notre Dame. The 20+ underdog Tulsa won at Notre Dame, a game Kirk Herbstreit as the greatest upset in all of college football for 2010 season!

2013 ASU vs. USC. In a game at Sun Devil Stadium, the underdog ASU team won in a 62–41 blowout, most points given up by USC in a game in USC football history.

2013 ASU vs UCLA. In this game, ASU upset UCLA to clinch the PAC 12 South championship

2014 ASU vs. USC. The underdog ASU team won at the Coliseum on the last play of the game, "the Jael Mary"

2014 ASU vs Notre Dame. The underdog Sun Devils won at Sun Devil Stadium, 55–31.

The 2017 ASU team, a huge underdog, upset top five in the nation Washington at Sun Devil Stadium.

Why Do We Love Wins by Underdogs So Much?

We love underdogs because they:

- **inspire** us.
- **capture** our attention.
- **win** because of character, discipline, and effort, not just natural ability.
- **pour** their hearts out for a common goal.
- **are humble team players!**

Of course, we adore them. Not matter our status, we should emulate them every day! We all can be better humans. Underdogs give us the model to propel ourselves to a new level.

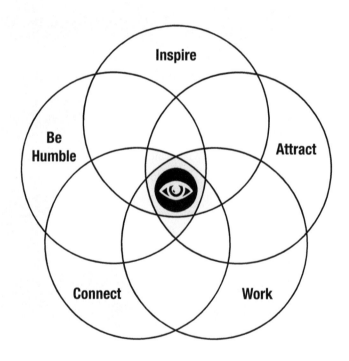

ADVENTURE: CREATE A CULTURE OF INNOVATION

Part of being a great coach is being a great innovator. Todd loves to figure out ways to stay ahead of the game. He likes to say that innovation has played a huge part in his success, and he is right. His basic core values of "character, intelligence, discipline, and toughness" are the foundations on which he builds his innovation. These core values give his players the ability to operate faster and more efficiently than the players on other teams, allowing them to cognitively handle more in a fast-paced and time-sensitive game. Speed in thought, along with physical speed, allows Todd to develop, train, and prepare his players better than those of his opponent.

That is not enough to win, either on the football field or in life. Todd likes to say—and I agree with him 100 percent—that most—nine out of ten—college football teams are copycats, and we hear that every week on football broadcasts: "It's a copycat league." Copycats do not win championships; that rarefied air is reserved for those who innovate. You must have a detailed overall plan that is designed for your specific personnel and values in order to win championships.

By being high-tech in the training room, in the classroom, and in the boardroom, you gain one advantage over the competition. Learning to think quickly, grasping the latest technology, and being nimbler than your opponents—these are all qualities that innovation gives you. I have seen Todd use this with great success for his players.

Innovation is empty, though, without spiritual direction and development. The core value of successful human beings is that we are all a part of something larger than ourselves. For Todd and me, our belief in and worship of God gives us the heart, direction, and motivation to serve and love others above our own wants and needs. If you want to live a championship life, it is critical to make time daily to focus on connecting with your spiritual purpose. **The spiritual development that guides us all gives us the motivation and inspiration and confidence to innovate and find better ways to serve others, so that those around us can share in the fruits of our labors.**

Innovation comes from adapting our training and schemes yearly in order to improve the skills and talents of the players we have and the ones we recruit. The most critical place for innovation is in personnel. We are innovative in recruiting because we want to recruit disciplined, highly intelligent players who are football smart and fit our core values. This allows us to be more advanced in tempo and planning than our opponents. We can operate faster and more efficiently than our opponents because we have a higher level of discipline, along with short- and long-range plans to develop and recruit disciplined and smart personnel.

> *"I've been around for a while and I've seen many great leaders, including national leaders. Todd Graham is one of the top five leaders that I have ever known in my life."*
> —Pastor Jack Graham

It goes back to the core value of serving others and sacrificing for others. That is the difference between just having a life and really living. The innate human desire to make things better is based on the belief that we all are part of something greater than just ourselves. True victory and fulfillment in life come in the service of others. You are a giver or a taker, bright-eyed or dull-eyed, a victor or a victim, grateful or entitled—those are your daily choices. So, live your life in the service of others, and you can't lose!

This philosophy of innovation is seen in the mission statements, values, and purpose established and propagated within highly successful corporations and organizations.

When I was working in education, we had words that drove us to be better and guide our innovation. The first ones I remember were "Whatever it takes," which propelled us into leadership role in education. The next were Rigor, Relationships, and Relevance. These three Rs helped us build an incredibly innovative curriculum for our students. For Todd's programs, it is Character, Smart, Discipline, Tough. You will see these words throughout this book. These words are the engine that drives change, growth, success, and champions. As you can see there is nothing about how many games will be won, yards will be gained and takeaways there will be because innovation is driven most strongly by people who have a mission beyond themselves or organizations.

Here are a few corporate examples of how they plan to change the world.

- **IKEA:** To create a better everyday life for the many people.
- **JetBlue:** To inspire humanity – both in the air and on the ground.
- **Tesla:** To accelerate the world's transition to sustainable energy.
- **TED:** Spread ideas.

Build a Culture of Innovation

- **Select** disciplined and smart people.
- **Research** and know your competition.
- **Use** the best tools available.
- **Create** purpose beyond the organization.
- **Build** fast, efficient, and flexible operations.

MIRACLE: LET EDUCATION LIFT YOU!

Educational Stories from Friends, Fans, and Family

Stacey Kampe: My husband Kenny hated school growing up. He dropped out his freshman year to work on the farm. He always told me school was too hard and he would never go back! He decided to get his GED at the age of fifty-two and then graduated from Scottsdale Community College with his associate's degree in general education! It was an incredible experience for him!

Justin Shuman: Before I met my wife, I lived a life of partying, drinking, and smoking in a small town that I was stuck in. My wife told me I was really smart and needed to enroll at ASU and make something of myself. She helped me to believe in the man I am today. It saved me from alcoholism and depression; not just that, but it instilled a confidence in me that I never knew I had. Growing up, I was afraid of failure, but failing in college and being picked back up by my new surrounding friends and family really made failure not seem so bad, and that it's okay to fall. Just keep getting back up.

Kristen Sullivan: I'm a stay-at-home mom, and although I never put my studies to use in the traditional sense, going to school and learning has taught me the importance of continuing to learn always and that it impacts your life in all aspects.

Janice Hansen: Education has drastically changed my life in myriad ways! I am the first of my family to graduate from college, and the first doctor in my family. I got my undergraduate degree at ASU. It was a place where I was able to thrive and experience many pivotal moments, including meeting my future spouse. Eighteen years later, we were back at ASU, dropping our daughter off for her first year as a Sun Devil. It was through her that we met the Grahams. Our daughter Alyssa was captain of the color guard, and Coach Graham was adamant that the marching band was just as much a part of the game-day experience as the players. There was no elitism in his program. The players were expected to treat the band, the spirit line, the groundskeepers, the fans—everyone who walked into the athletics building—respectfully. He even brought the marching band out from under the music department and into athletics, which opened up a whole new world to kids who work extremely hard for very little support in most arenas. It seems like such a little thing, but it truly made a huge difference for my daughter, because she realized her role was just as important to the game-day experience as any player's. Coach Graham made the choice to go out into the community on a summer outreach called the Sun Devil Caravan. At these events, coaches and players would board a bus and travel to different areas of Arizona and California. There, they'd do a service event as well as a school outreach pep rally. In the evening, they'd meet with alumni and supporters of Sun Devil athletics. Coach Graham insisted on the service part of these adventures. My daughter saw what was going on and thought that since she was part of the athletic department, perhaps she could be one of the students who pitched in as well. This led to a fantastic partnership where band members were included right alongside the players and coaches. Kids who participated the events could see many different types of people going to college and found themselves reflected in band kids as well as athletes. It was a huge success and really made my daughter's experience at ASU wonderful.

Vi Teofilo: Coach Graham always ingrained in us the importance of getting a degree, sometimes going out of his way to ensure our success in the classroom.

Trent Figg: When coaching at Southern Arkansas University, I had several young men who were first-generation college students. Seeing the joy in their eyes and the pride from their parents upon graduation was truly life changing.

Tracy Sanders: Education for me changed my life by meeting my husband, Tim, in my night class that I was taking at SCC. We both were taking a human sexuality class, and he sat behind me. One evening we were waiting for class to start and he started talking to me, and from there it was just the beginning of a relationship and now twenty years later, a marriage.

Curnelius Arnick: Education has definitely changed the course of my life. I am the first male in my family to graduate from college.

I have challenged myself to continue setting the bar high for my little brother, cousin, and anyone who looks up to me as a positive influence in their life. I was blessed to leave TU with two degrees: business management and marketing. In 2017 I graduated from the University of Dallas with my master's in business administration. Without education, the career that I have developed at the Federal Reserve would be nearly impossible to achieve. Before I left TU, I challenged my teammates to make sure they left with their degrees. Playing football was great, but as we all know, that must come to an end someday. However, obtaining a great education is something that will last a lifetime. Between parties, practices, and NFL dreams, oftentimes we forget about the big picture. A harsh reality that so many athletes fail to realize is that colleges use them for their athletic ability. A golden rule that I believe is that athletes should use the school to get everything they can from it before their time at the university is over. If the athlete leaves that school without a degree or two, then they have done a disservice to themselves. One person who comes to mind my brother, Shawn Jackson. He told me that those words I shared on senior night really helped push him to get this degree from TU. I was glad to know that I was able [to] motivate someone to take advantage of the opportunities that were in front of us.

Shannon Carter: It gave me the opportunity to have a career of choice and not have to settle for a job.

Amy Smalley: I believe education was the starting point for big change in my life. I met Michael, my husband, at Baylor University. I struggled to make the decision on what college to attend. God led me to Baylor as I prayed where I would best fit. If I hadn't gone to Baylor, I wouldn't have met my sweetheart! The community of college changed me as well. It was the right mix of responsibility and freedom that matured me beyond the scope my parents could provide.

Lauren Depew: As a freshman in college, I was struggling with my classes and grades. It wasn't because it was too hard; it was because I was unmotivated. I felt like I was wasting my time on a college degree because I knew I wanted to be a mom, but my dad insisted it was beneficial. It wasn't until I took a trip to Uganda that I had the realization that my education wasn't about me at all. As soon as I got back, I transferred to a university that had a nonprofit management program, and I graduated three years later. My education wasn't a waste of time; it was an open door to change the world.

Melissa Cohen: My ASU education is the most valuable achievement in my life. As my mom told me, it's the one thing nobody will ever be able to take away from me. The fact that I am a Sun Devil also afforded me the opportunity to meet the Grahams—a huge blessing!

Walter Boyd: I was the first person in my family to go to and graduate from college. Coach Graham told me, "You are changing the minimum expectation for your children and your family."

TENACIOUS SMART SUMMARY

Match your sacrifices to your goals.

Select personnel with detail and creativity.

Communicate daily—Speak Victory!

Adapt and design system for skills of personnel.

Implement seamless integration of technology.

Plan to Teach and Teach to Plan.

Research and Process.

Be a Victor, not a Victim.

Promote an atmosphere of continuous learning

Focus on innovation and creativity.

Remember, if you miss the worst of times, you will also miss the best of times.

Play Smart!

"Complexity in organization makes simplicity for operations."
- Tom Landry

STRIVE TO CONTINUOUSLY IMPROVE

TENACIOUS DISCIPLINE

PERFORM **EVERY DAY** **EVERY MINUTE** AS **CHAMPIONS!**

PLAYBOOK

THE GRAHAM GAME PLAN

OPPOSITION'S DISCIPLINE STRATEGY

THE DISCIPLINE CALL SHEET: 7 C's

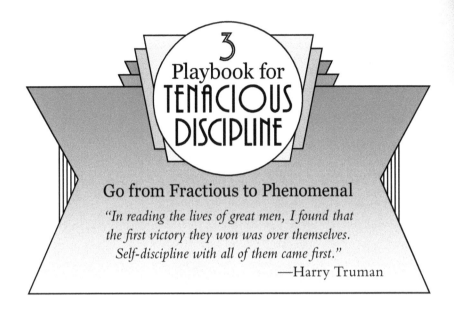

3

Playbook for
TENACIOUS DISCIPLINE

Go from Fractious to Phenomenal

"In reading the lives of great men, I found that the first victory they won was over themselves. Self-discipline with all of them came first."

—Harry Truman

WHAT CAN MARSHMALLOWS TEACH US ABOUT SELF-DISCIPLINE?

Almost fifty years ago, "The Stanford Marshmallow Experiment" taught us about self-discipline. It offered kids a snack, then told them if they waited to eat the snack, they would get two snacks!

It turned out that the result offered a simple way to predict the future of a child. Researchers were able to predict academic and social competence as well as weight and stress levels. Self-discipline plays a critical role in every aspect of our lives. For the most part, those who can wait for the marshmallow experience better relationships and greater success. It isn't what we would all like to enjoy, but we have to learn the power and payoff of discipline.

The GRAHAM Game Plan for Tenacious Discipline

GOAL: Become a disciplined champion.

RELATIONSHIP: Play prevent.

AGENCY: Be ready to intercept.

HABITS: Release the monkeys.

ADVENTURE: One plus one equals one.

MIRACLE: Create a championship team.

Opposition's Discipline Strategy

Fracture Your Personality and Relationships with Chaos.

Your personality and relationships will be fractured if your life is dominated by the following:

Neglect those you love.

Continue the cycle of **ignorance**.

Make rash emotionally-filled **choices**.

Fill your mind with **self-doubt and insecurity**.

Lack ambition and perspective.

Leave your **fate** to others.

Get stuck in a **rut**.

Torture yourself with **unforgiveness**.

Disrespect other people's needs.

The 7 C's Discipline Call Sheet: Take Action

1. Be Compassionate.
Fight for forgiveness.

2. Be Captivating.
Selflessness samples.

3. Be Commanding.
Do you have any monkeys?
Turn off autopilot.

4. Be Committed.
Make a promise, not perfection.
Use tools for becoming one.

5. Be Connected.
Giving is receiving.
Find a friend instead of a foe.
R-E-S-P-E-C-T.

6. Be Courageous.
Learn a new language.

7. Be Creative.
Adapt your strategy.
Use offensive and defensive strategies for marriage.
Create your own fairy-tale marriage.

GOAL: BECOME A DISCIPLINED CHAMPION

Over the years I have encountered this great poem, "Autobiography in Five Short Chapters," written by Portia Nelson. It reminds me of how we can get stuck in unhealthy patterns that prevent us from growing into our best selves at work and home.

The Parable of the Hole

Chapter One

I walk down the street.
There is a deep hole in the sidewalk.
I fall in.
I am lost ... I am helpless.
It isn't my fault.
It takes forever to find a way out.

Chapter Two

I walk down the same street.
There is a deep hole in the sidewalk.
I pretend I don't see it.
I fall in again.
I can't believe I'm in the same place.
But, it isn't my fault.
It still takes a long time getting out.

Chapter Three

I walk down the same street.
There is a deep hole in the sidewalk.
I see it is there.
I still fall in ... it's a habit ... but,
my eyes are open.
I know where I am.
It is *my* fault.
I get out immediately.

Chapter Four
I walk down the same street.
There is a deep hole in the sidewalk.
I walk around it.

Chapter Five
I walk down another street.[1]

There are many streets we walk down in life: getting married, raising a family, building a professional career, being active in a church, being active in local politics, contributing to a community, being active in a sport, and so on. Each of these streets has its unique holes that we can fall into, preventing our progress down the street and destroying our potential for success. In marriage, the holes seem to include the following for every couple: spending too much money, depression, lying, trying to control your husband or wife, refusing to take responsibility for your mistakes, getting angry when the situation does not require anger, and letting your partner make all of your decisions. In each of these areas, we can either learn from our mistakes and take another path or keep falling into the same holes over and over.

For Todd and me, there was a great irony in our marriage. We tended to adapt to change easily in our professional lives but not in our love lives. We did everything we could to be champions in life, but we fell into negative patterns in our love lives: doing the same things over and over yet expecting different results. We do not have the same courage or disciplined approach to success in marriage. **It's as if the human heart gets stuck in traps within a marriage while the human mind learns to avoid these traps on the field or in the office.** At first, Todd and I did not know how to avoid these traps at home, but we also did not want our children to fall into the same patterns of behavior. It took many years of research, with additional advice from our friends, pastors, and marriage counselors, to learn what we were doing and how to turn our marriage from struggling to sacred. **To achieve greatness at the office, on the field, or at home, we must become disciplined champions.**

---

[1] Nelson, Portia. "Autobiography in Five Short Chapters," *There's a Hole in My Sidewalk: The Romance of Self-Discovery*, New York: Atria Paperback, 2012

*"Married life is easy, and it's just like a walk in the park.
But the problem is that the park is* Jurassic Park.
—Internet meme

Joining the Circus

In *Jurassic Park,* people "play God" by creating living creatures they cannot control, using technology they don't fully understand. This theme translates directly to marriage: when you get married, you are creating a living creature—the marriage—that you cannot fully understand at the beginning because each person in the marriage will change and grow over time. You cannot control the other person in the marriage, but you can control yourself, and if you don't control yourself properly, you will be responsible through your actions and inaction for destroying the marriage. By learning to control your responses to your spouse and to your children, you can save your marriage, your children, and yourself.

Just as in *Jurassic Park*, the best and worst behaviors of each partner in a marriage will amplify with repetition, turning even the smallest features of the husband and wife into large creatures that you must learn to control. In *Jurassic Park* the creatures are dinosaurs, including velociraptors and a tyrannosaurus rex. However, in real life marriage is more like a zoo in which the animals are either safely in cages because you control them or on your back if you do not control them. You enter the marriage with love, hope, and optimism, just as you enter the zoo with love for the animals and optimism that you will have a great interaction with them. As your marriage expands with children, disagreements, arguments, and make-up sessions, your love will be tested, your hope may fade, and your optimism may turn into despair. If that happens, you are no longer looking at animals in a zoo. Instead, the animals are on your back. These animals are there to deceive, disrupt, and destroy anything that might be good in your relationships and organizations. The most destructive animals create hopelessness.

In our case, the animals were the proverbial monkeys on our back. However, we did not create an ordinary zoo. When your life is coaching football, interacting with football players, supporting programs and people, and dealing with stepfamilies, constant moves, a child custody case, financial stress, and more, the zoo becomes a circus. **In a zoo the animals are safely separated from you and your family**. In a circus the animals must perform for even larger audiences, and they are not always caged. Todd and I created not only a marriage but an instant family by combining our five children and adding one more. We even adopted numerous people along the way as temporary family members, in addition to the thousands of visitors and thousands of dinner guests. All this change resulted in much discomfort and pain. Our home had more going on than a three-ring circus, with me as the ringmaster! Through reorganization, retooling, reinventing, and revising, I was forced to become the most effective ringmaster, not only at home but at the stadium where my husband lived almost full-time during the season.

Over the years, I learned to be an effective ringmaster and to make sure the monkeys in our life stayed in their cages instead of climbing onto our backs. But in the beginning these monkeys were climbing all over us.

We both came in with lots of baggage that filled every room in our home, then we added the stressors from Todd's coaching career. The divorce rate of college football coaches is high to begin with. I have heard that 70 to 85 percent of college football coaches are divorced. With the long hours, the absence from important events, the pressure of the job on the whole family, and multiple other factors of the coaching profession, the odds of a successful marriage were against us. We had each come into our marriage with complications and complexities that brought us to the edge of divorce many times. **We can all have terrible thoughts, mangled motivations, pride, and fear that deprive us of our best.** Now, after decades, Todd and I both say our marriage is our most significant achievement, one we have fought hard for, because our marriage has been the foundation for all of our other accomplishments. By becoming disciplined champions, we learned how to get off merry-go-round and start walking down new streets and manage our monkeys.

The Cycle of Anger

In our marriage, the hole we kept jumping into was the merry-go-round.

"When you're on a merry-go-round, you miss a lot of the scenery."
—Neil Diamond[2]

Getting Off the Merry-Go-Round

The cycle of anger is like a merry-go-round. Like its companion emotion fear, anger makes us focus only on the thing we are angry about. By focusing on that one thing, we can easily miss the events that might fix the problem—the scenery that's whizzing by as we stare incessantly at the center of the merry-go-round. This is the problem especially with righteous anger. We get so busy defending the righteousness of a cause that we can easily overlook evidence that the cause is being addressed through effective efforts. It is important, even in the midst of anger, make efforts to fix the problem that triggered the anger.

At one point in our life together, **the merry-go-round started feeling normal, except I felt a constant sense of vertigo and motion sickness.**

---

[2] Robert Windeler, "This Diamond Is Forever," *People*, January 22, 1979

Todd and I were lucky because we were both able to recognize this cycle and stop it before it did too much damage to our marriage. However, we went through this cycle many times in the first ten years of our marriage. The merry-go-round was the hole Todd and I kept falling into as we walked down the street of marriage. It was our normal in the first few years. It became a weekly occurrence. It diminished the trust and transparency in our marriage. As we sought to salvage our family, our first goal was getting off the merry-go-round.

As the years passed, we learned to stop pushing the buttons that started the merry-go-round, so we avoided escalation. We both took responsibility. Some days Todd took our conversation back to a positive place, and other days I took my finger off the button. During times of extreme stress, we would start the cycle again, but after the tenth year our rides on the merry-go-round became shorter as we learned to avoid this particular hole on the street called marriage. Indeed, last year, I was tempted to get on the merry-go-round of anger once again, but I chose to walk down a new road by releasing all the pain and contempt that made me get angry in the first place. We did not get on the crazy merry-go-round.

At the beginning of our marriage, I did not have the skills to even avoid the hole. As the years passed, I learned to get out of the hole quickly and then to avoid falling into it. This did not happen overnight. It took years of courage and discipline. But a great football player does not become great overnight either. Every great player endures years of practice and discipline in order to become a champion athlete in their game, no matter what the game is. It is important that we avoid trying to achieve overnight success. The story about the tortoise and the hare is true in marriage too: slow and steady always wins!

RELATIONSHIP: PLAY PREVENT

The Best Offense Is a Good Defense

Many football players and coaches adopt the saying "the best defense is a good offense."

I learned over the years that football is really about playing good defense, and this is true for marriage as well. When you are playing good defense, you are preventing the other team from scoring more than focusing on scoring a goal. A prevent defense is a defensive alignment that prevents the other team from making a big play. Todd lives this motto. I used to wear an old T-shirt from his closet that said, "The best offense is a great defense." Todd obviously knew how to create a great defense on the football field, but I do not think either of us realized how important it is to have defensive strategies in marriage.

I think the world wants to destroy families. I have witnessed the attacks. The church gave us sound advice about how to protect our marriage, how to play good defense. **A perfect marriage is not one without conflicts; it is full of them.** Our faith got us through the toughest times in our marriage because of the enormous wisdom we gained from reading and listening to God's Word and from church families who supported us during trials. The church family and neighborhood group gave us positive emotional support and practical wisdom while providing us with honest, mature advice.

Our memories with Coach and Penni have been in our Monday night Bible studies. We have shared so much in that time with the tough decisions in life over so many prayers and praising the moments God has blessed us and healed us. Learning God's Word together has brought us together as a family, and we are so grateful for that. —Tracy Sanders

Make a Promise, Not Perfection

One amazing resource was Christian counseling.

Christian counseling is very different from traditional counseling. In traditional counseling, the focus is on being the perfect partner for the other person. Todd and I would never be perfect for each other, so we would never have persisted. Traditional counseling and marriage courses also seem to ignore the requirements and adversity of nontraditional professions. My husband is not going to sit down and have a heart-to-heart talk with me every evening. He will not have dinner with me every night. I didn't even expect this from him. There are other professions that pose the same limitations for spouses, including those of preachers, soldiers, medical doctors, corporate executives, investment brokers, and real estate brokers among other specialized and high-risk professions. The women I met whose spouses or they are in these professions became some of my closest friends. We each understand the pressures the others face and judgement from those who do not understand. Many of us have grown tired of explaining why our families are not together at 6 p.m. each night for dinner and why I cannot commit to an event because we simply do not know what the future brings.

In contrast to traditional counseling, **Christian counseling is about putting the marriage first.** Being committed to marriage is a different construct than being the best possible partner for the other person. Our relationship turned into being about loving each other, not merely about doing things to make the other person happy. As soon as we made this switch, I felt the stability and safety I craved so deeply, and Todd felt the respect and honor most men desire from marriage. This switch changed our relationship completely. Through our commitment to our marriage, our behaviors changed. We no longer experienced the pressure of doing things to prove ourselves to each other or the failure caused by not meeting expectations because our unpredictable life.

You don't just try to put love points on your spouse's heart like a football team aggressively trying to put points on the board and try to make certain that you are ahead on the scoreboard. You express your love to your spouse in ways that make both of you happy when possible and with freedom, knowing you are committed to marriage. Playing prevent means your relationship isn't just about making touchdowns and your performance on the field; instead, it is about a disciplined commitment to the team on and off the field. This applies to every aspect of life. If your only goal at work is being top sales person and you aren't committed to the corporate team, your success will most likely be short lived.

Offensive and Defensive Strategies for Marriage

 Do:

1. **Treat** your marriage as unique. The two of you are the only people who experience your marriage.
2. **Be** warm and affectionate toward your spouse.
3. **Be** open to intimate conversations.
4. Always be transparent with your spouse. **Tell** the truth.
5. Your spouse is smart and attentive. **Tell** your spouse about a task only once.
6. **Give** your spouse the benefit of the doubt whenever you perceive a mistake.
7. **Keep** your promises.
8. **Make** certain your spouse knows they are the most important person in your life.

♥ *Do not:*

1. **Compare** your marriage to others.
2. **Be** cold or withdrawn.
3. **Refuse** to discuss problems.
4. **Have** expectations that are too high or too low.
5. **Tell** white lies.
6. **Nag**.
7. **Ignore** your own ambitions.
8. **Blame**.
9. **Break** promises.

Adapting Your Strategy

As I mentioned previously, playing good defense in marriage is just like playing good defense in football. One of the foundations of football is strategy. The most common defensive front in football is a four-down front. Any opposing team will expect this and plan for this formation in their offensive front. The best way to form a defensive strategy is to throw the opposing team off their game with an odd-stack defense. Todd started working on an odd-stack defense while he coached the University of West Virginia. He collaborated with the assistant defensive coach to develop different odd-stack lineups. "By moving to a three-down front we were … unique in our attack. … taking away a defensive lineman and adding a more athletic football player allows you to have more speed at eight positions on the field. This was also more helpful in defending the rising dominance of spread offenses where the offensive personnel were also built for speed."

According to Todd, the odd stack helped him recruit high school football players because "typically your average high school football team has more mid-skill and skill players than defensive lineman. [This] allows high school and college coaching to maximize [player] potential by adapting their attack based on the skills and talents available." So, these are the advantages of defensive planning on the back end, recruitment. There are also advantages on the front end, game play. "By standing one more guy up you are allowed to be more versatile, adding to coverage, or pressures, and blitz from additional second and third level positions." This ability to add coverage to different positions requires different protection rules for opponent offenses.

Upset of the Year!

Todd and Penni Graham

Todd demonstrated the effectiveness of the prevent defense over the years with his players. When Todd coached Tulsa against Notre Dame on October 30, 2010, a single defensive action by Tulsa helped them win an upset victory, 28–27, the biggest win in the history of the school. The setting was unique. We had lost the first game of the year to East Carolina on a Hail Mary, the last play of the game. However, we won five of the next six games. We played the eighth game of the year against Notre Dame, at Notre Dame. We were the twenty-one-point underdog. No one gave us much chance going in against the Irish at home on their turf.

In the week leading up to the game we put in hours of work. We had smart players, and so we were able to do a lot schematically. We wanted to use our speed, quickness, and smarts against them. We also benefited from the fact that our guys were hungry to go in there and win. We went into the game with a fast, explosive team. We believed we could beat anyone.

Todd coached confidently and aggressively. In the opening drive Tulsa scored their only offensive touchdown of the game. It was a very low-scoring game, but we had great strategic planning. We attacked with our defensive front. Notre Dame attempted a quick passing game, and they were succeeding, taking a 20–12 second quarter lead. However, Tulsa deflected the ball, and Shawn Jackson picked it off, going sixty-six yards for a touchdown, cutting Notre Dame's lead at halftime to two points, 20–18.

The key to the game was Tulsa's championship defense. Tulsa had three interceptions and no turnovers. The team knew that if they started winning on offense, the game would be ours. The mantra was to not beat ourselves: no turnovers, no penalties.

In the third quarter Tulsa made the big play: Damaris Johnson returned a punt for fifty-nine yards and a touchdown, for a score of 27–25, Notre Dame. Finally, in the fourth quarter, at third and twenty-six, G. J. Kinne, the quarterback for Tulsa, threw to Ricky Johnson for thirty-one yards, first down, and finally a twenty-seven-yard field goal. Kevin Fitzpatrick scored three points for Tulsa, putting Tulsa ahead 28–27. Tulsa kicked off with three minutes and twenty-three seconds left in the game. Since Tulsa was winning, all Tulsa had to do for the remainder of the clock was stop Notre Dame from scoring.

Notre Dame's drive toward the end zone was strong, going to third down three times and converting them all. They made it to Tulsa's nineteen-yard line. I was sitting on the side of the end zone crying. All Notre Dame had to do was kick a short field goal to win. They had Michael Floyd, one of the best receivers in the country, going against our 170-pound cornerback John Flanders. Tulsa was bluffing like we were bringing pressure. Notre Dame attempted a fade route to Floyd, but Flanders stepped up in the end zone and intercepted the ball with thirty-six seconds left on the clock. It was one of the most incredible plays in one of the most miraculous moments. I've never seen a group of young man show so much heart and character. Tulsa won the Kirk Herbstreit award for the biggest upset that season.

Championship Teams Cultivate and Communicate for Change

Just as Todd had to adapt his defensive strategy, in marriage we constantly need to be aware of ways we need to adapt. Families are ever-changing, so we must be looking for ways to adapt in order to keep our marriages healthy and growing. If you aren't moving forward, you are moving backward. Change is part of marriage. Cultivating change promotes healthy growth. Part of having a good defense in your marriage is making plans for long-term success. Our marriage improves each year; it grows as we grow as people. As a coach, you are constantly cultivating change, sometimes during half time. If your losing, you cannot expect to keep the same game plan and win. Most of halftime is spent talking about changes to the game plan.

Communicating changing needs and desires keeps your marriage fresh and at times fascinating. When we got married, I did not like getting flowers, but Todd continued to send them. He got the hint about five years later. However, I changed. I grew to love having fresh flowers in my house when I would host parties and events. Ten years later, I went back to my husband with my new desire to receive flowers. He loves going to our local Safeway and working with the flower lady to find a special vase and flowers for me. At times in our marriage, I have expected my husband to read my mind. What a disaster! His gifts for our anniversary ranged from purses with overly extravagant prices (two years in row), sixty dollars' worth of L'Oreal makeup from CVS, to a plastic-framed picture of Jesus. I carried open pens and chicken nuggets in my purse, so I would not want an expensive purse. He was so excited to bring home the French makeup that I had probably never heard of. I hung the picture of Jesus over Michael's bed.

The best defense in marriage is clearly communicating in a variety of ways because sometimes we have different communication styles. And we need to communicate more than once, because in our information overload society our brains do not always take in all the information all the time. **Be disciplined in your communication; cultivate change instead of just reacting to it.**

 **The Four Ws and the H of Communication**

Who you are,

What you desire,

When can we talk,

Why you love them, and

How you want to live?

AGENCY: BE READY TO INTERCEPT

The interception that won the game for Tulsa is like the interception each of us must make to win the game of marriage. When you show love, forgiveness, and affection to your spouse, you make a touchdown because only you can make your partner feel like the most special person in the world. But remember, for every expression of love you show to your spouse, there are equal amounts of anger and jealousy that can creep into your heart to break your love connection. **You must play good defense, blocking anger and jealousy from entering your heart.** The best way to stop negative emotions from entering your heart is to intercept them before they get into the end zone that is your soul. There is a saying, "No one can make you feel inferior without your consent." It is the same in marriage: no one can make you angry and jealous toward your spouse unless you allow these emotions into your heart. If you play a good prevent game, then these emotions will never enter your heart.

An interception happens whenever someone from the opposing team captures the ball after it is thrown to a player on your team. An interception is almost impossible to avoid if the timing isn't right: a ball thrown a little too early or too late can land in the opposing team's hands instead of the intended hands. No amount of strategy can account for chance—the possibility that the thrown ball will be off by a few feet or that an opposing team player will jump at just the right moment to catch the ball. An interception is thus one of the best ways to play a prevent defense. Coaches build strategies and schemes to create the best opportunities for players to intercept the ball, and players are coached to stay alert and watch the quarterback's eyes, the receiver's route, and the ball so they can position themselves to make an interception. Making the interception starts with having the discipline to practice all this daily. I do not believe there has ever been a championship team that did not work consistently on intercepting the ball. How do we make interceptions at home and at work?

Strategies for Making Interceptions off the Field

1. Create strategies to block negative actions and reactions.
2. Be alert to all aspects of a relationship or a workplace.
3. Be physically, mentally, and emotionally prepared.
4. Practice daily.

"The Hawaii Bowl when we played Hawaii on Christmas Eve. Our team was excited to be over there to enjoy such a beautiful place. On game day, we were focused like never before. We completely destroyed them in their own stadium. Our defense was playing lights out. We had maybe four or five picks that game. I had two picks myself, which I returned one for a TD and the other I got tackled at the one-yard line."

—Curnelius Arnick

Interceptions That Changed Our Games

1. Everyone was out of their seats. The smallest school in the nation was beating Notre Dame 28–27 on their home field, but Notre Dame managed to push their way down to the Tulsa nineteen-yard line with less than a minute left. Notre Dame could merely kick a field goal to win the game. Coach Kelly thought it was a sure bet to put Michael Floyd, one of the biggest and best receivers in college football, against Tulsa's 5'9"corner John Flanders. You could hear the air being knocked out of Notre Dame as John reached up and grabbed the ball before it got to Michael Floyd's hands.

2. The year before, ASU had a heartbreaking loss to Notre Dame. This year, it was different story. With less than four minutes left in the game, Lloyd Carrington sealed the win. As the ball bounced off the 6'4" Robinson's hands, Lloyd took the ball to the house with a fifty-eight-yard touchdown! This pushed ASU's lead to 48–31. Final score: 55–31!

3. The Pac-12 South, the Territorial Cup, and much more were on the line. Damarious Randall had his eyes focused on the ball. With his lightning speed and agility, he intercepted the ball just as it was about to land in the receiver's hands. Unstoppable, Damarious ran thirty-eight yards untouched to score, giving ASU the 37–14 lead they needed to seal their win!

4. Tied 34–34 at Cal with just three minutes left, Zane Gonzalez kicked a field goal to give ASU a 37–34 lead. ASU fans took deep breath, and then Liau Moeakiola picked off the ball from Webb and scored a twenty-eight-yard touchdown. The Sun Devil Stadium was rocking! Todd and his defensive staff had talked all week about forcing more turnovers. To build on Liau's success, D. J. Calhoun, untouched, returned Cal's onside kick for a forty-two-yard touchdown.

5. Aldon Darby ran with a forty-six-yard interception to give more of lead for ASU against USC. This amazing defensive strategy was what was needed for ASU to win the game.

6. With a game where the offenses combined to rack up over 1000 yards, the defense made the blow that took ASU to a win over USC. USC started the third quarter with a lead. The next forty-seven seconds changed everything. First, Taylor Kelly threw a seventy-four-yard touchdown pass to D. J. Foster to take the game over. Alden Darby then stuck a knife in the heart of USC by intercepting Cody Kessler's pass and running forty-six yards for a touchdown, giving ASU a thirteen-point lead.

HABIT: RELEASE THE MONKEYS

Remember when I mentioned our circus? We had barrel of monkeys in our circus. Their favorite place to hang was on our backs. The monkeys on our backs come from past relationships. We bring our past into all of our relationships. Growing up in entirely different kinds of crazy families made it even worse for and me—the yelling in his house, the silence in mine. Besides our childhood and adult challenges, we added multiple marriages, stepfamilies, a crazy career, financial difficulties, moving over and over, and child custody cases. Of course, we always had extra people living with us to add to the chaos. One day I counted that we had over thirty different people living with us over a ten-year period, not including family, two people I had never met! One of my girlfriends observed my lifestyle and gave me a necklace that said, "Breathe."

The Monkey Called Blame

The huge amount of stress and responsibility forced us to live in frustration and blame. **We faced so much adversity from so many directions that we could not in good conscience let our pain out on others. Instead, we let our pain out on each other.** The pain included regrets from the past, blame for the present, and contempt for each other as we each expressed doubt about the other person's ability to be there for us in the future. We were stuck in contradiction because we both viewed blame as something the weak did, a tool the weak use to avoid personal responsibility, but we both regularly blamed each other. We had accomplished so much together and done so much for so many. Yet instead of seeing the greatness in each other, we saw only each other's faults, ignoring our own individual faults. Even if we had acknowledged our individual faults, we would have been too proud and refused to ask each other, even God, for forgiveness.

For this reason, I consider the biggest monkey in our relationship to be the blame we expressed toward each other and family members.

 **The Impact of Blame**

Blame can destroy all levels relationships and organization with its impact. It

- **Stops** growth, severely damages relationships.
- **Creates** a victim mentality.
- **Feeds** the ego by telling you that a problem is always someone else's fault, absolving you of all responsibility.
- **Kills** healthy relationships.

Todd and I both had to get rid of this monkey, so we had to stop blaming each other.

To start eliminating the blame, I did something important to me: I told Todd we had enough long-term guests, so we could not take any more. Having additional people in our home cut the amount of time we had together as a family, increased our expenses, forced us to consider our guests in our plans, and reduced time for intimacy in all ways. Todd heard my distress and agreed with me. I am forever grateful to him for our shared victory over this monkey. We reduced the number of long-term guests living with us, which reduced the stress and conflict and, as a consequence, the blame. We simplified our lives. Simplicity is so often the answer to ridding ourselves of monkeys.

The Monkey Named Grudge

Now to the next monkey: Todd came into our marriage from a family that practiced forgiveness as action, not as spoken words. Even though "I am sorry" was rarely spoken when Todd was growing up, I swear his family had a five-second rule regarding forgiveness. They could be screaming at each other or even in fist fights, and it would just end. The next words communicated would be something like, "What do you want to eat?" This meant all was forgiven, and everyone was moving on.

In our marriage I had a three-day rule, not a five-second rule. I would be in angst with worry about something for days. He would often walk in the door and say, "Hi, Baby!" and I would growl. Over time I watched and learned that I was only hurting myself. I was walking around having a pity party, irritated, and not enjoying life because, in my mind, he had to pay for whatever I was angry about.

However, I was the one who was paying. **Grudges kept my mind and heart jailed in contempt and sadness.** I had the choice to be set free or to stay in prison. I was in a slow-release program. By breaking the chains of grudges and blame, I found peace I had not enjoyed in decades. Since I was the one who created the chains, I was the only one who could break them. The only person I can change is myself. **Agency is key to finding peace. We control our inner lives. We decide how to feel.**

Fighting for Forgiveness

Now to the next monkey: I thought we had gotten rid of all our monkeys, but I was wrong. It seemed as if the older the monkey is, the more difficulty we had forcing it to leave. Logic does not apply here. I would think the most recent grudge would hold on the most, but **the oldest grudges proved to be the most powerful.** I now understand that the longer we have a memory, the deeper it goes into the brain, so a deep sense of self-efficacy and commitment is required to change the brain from blame to forgiveness.

Many people seek happiness in marriage, or we chase money, fame, things, and a relationship, believing that they will bring us joy. However, I think the path to happiness, which I consider peace, is through the forgiveness of others and ourselves. If we are unwilling to forgive, our hearts feel tortured with contempt, jealousy, and anger.

There is no road to happiness without passage through forgiveness. I want to contribute peace to the world, but I can only give what I have. I cannot have peace without constantly renewing my heart and ridding it of any grudges that exist—forgiving over and over.

"Penni is one of the most forgiving people I've ever met. I have been in Penni's life thirty-five years, and I have seen situations that she could have held grudges or given up on people. Instead, she has shown grace and forgiveness."

—Pam Wakefield

Giving Is Receiving

I was blessed with multiple resources regarding forgiveness growing up. I spent most of my early years with my grandparents, who I think never had a cross word for anyone. We spent many days in a small church, and the other days we volunteered at the Veterans Administration hospital. We also volunteered at Dietert Claim, a retirement community that we supported by running a thrift shop. I think both volunteer opportunities gave me a deep sense of gratitude and taught me about serving others. Giving back gave me a great sense of purpose. These experiences gave me some of my favorite childhood memories. I think volunteering is one of the most powerful tools for any emotional distress. **Volunteering can remove jealousy, bitterness, and hostility.** Once these emotional obstacles are removed from your heart, you can find the path straight to forgiveness. My grandparents were also humble people. Humility is critical in the forgiveness process.

Humility isn't about looking at yourself with a lack of self-esteem or putting yourself down; it's about putting others ahead of yourself. It's about serving others with compassion, kindness, gentleness, and patience.

Any time I feel a sense of not being good enough or feel a pity party coming on, I go help someone. The change in my head and heart are immediate and amazing. For example, I had always wanted to be a CASA (Court-Appointed Special Advocate) for foster children, so about six years ago I finally did it. What I learned was invaluable, and the blessings I got from that changed my life forever. This year we're going on our first mission trip, to Belarus. Often people think of volunteering as only an act of giving. We don't always remember or maybe even realize what we are receiving.

👁 Rewards of Helping Others

Purpose. The act of helping others gives us a rewarding feeling. We feel as though we have made a difference, an impact. It is natural to want to feel wanted, and when you volunteer, you feel more than wanted; you feel needed.

Confidence. Have you ever felt a little insecure, as though you needed a confidence boost? We have all been there, but next time this happens to you, try volunteering for the day. When you see others in need and hear what horrors they have faced, you will automatically feel better about whatever insecurity was bothering you earlier.

Positivity. Take a look at your social circle. Would you consider yourself a positive friend? Is everyone in your group mostly negative? People who volunteer tend to be more positive. They feel grateful for everything that they are blessed with in life. You can take these positive vibes and spread them throughout your social circle. The more positive you are, the more people will want to be around you.

Inner Peace. So many times, people stress over finances, work, or a never-ending task list. We want to make it seem like we have it all together and that we know all of the answers. People's impressions are everything. But what if you didn't have to live like that? What if you could find inner peace with who you are and what you bring to the table? Volunteering can help with that, as it is known to reduce stress. It's okay to let go of the reins and relax. We don't have to have everything figured out.

I brought volunteering back into my life as a way to release the most difficult and obstinate monkeys. Sometimes we can get so wrapped up in our own lives that we forget everyone else. **Life is much bigger than just you. Volunteering can help keep life in perspective.**

 **Do You Have Any Monkeys?**

- What is the monkey? Monkeys can be any negative: money, envy, regret, laziness, worry, etc.
- Why did you invite the monkey into your home?
- Why are you letting the monkey stay?
- How does the monkey make you feel?

Talk to a friend about your monkey and ask them to help you take it back to the wild. Know that you are the only one who can get rid of the monkey.

Exchange Your Monkeys for Peace of Mind

Throughout my life, I had multiple family members attend a twelve-step program. As a result, I also entered and spent lots of time in various twelve-step programs, including Adult Children of Alcoholics and Al-Anon support groups for family and friends of alcoholics. Step eight (forgiveness or making amends) is almost always the hardest and must be visited over and over. In the process of forgiving someone, most people find they also need to ask for forgiveness. The program maintains that this is a critical step in removing fear and shame (*big* monkeys), allowing us to live life to the fullest. Twelve-step programs offer lots of materials on forgiveness and on making amends. They also provide many resources for either giving or asking for forgiveness, whether the targeted individual is living or deceased. There are a variety of ways to forgive or ask for forgiveness. Many people are afraid of the reaction when facing someone they have hurt, yet there are so many remarkable stories of healing for both parties.

The monkeys in our lives can cause extreme damage to our emotional, mental, and physical health. It is our responsibility to remove the monkeys. No one else can do this for us. There are many resources you can seek to help remove monkeys that are causing havoc in your life. As long as these monkeys are hanging around, you cannot have the peace that God intends for you to experience.

 "For God did not give us a spirit of fear, but of power and love and of a sound mind" (2 Timothy 1:7).

ADVENTURE: ONE PLUS ONE EQUALS ONE

Penni and Todd in Canada

> "As iron sharpens iron, so a man sharpens the
> countenance of his friend"(Proverbs 27:17).
> I think "iron-sharpening" has been a
> key component in our marriage.

"Love is a battlefield."
—Pat Benatar

Earlier I talked about how Todd and I became rivals because of our individual professional goals. Todd is such a competitor. **We had to work hard to keep competition out of our marriage and make it a win-win.** When we first married, every situation definitely felt more like a win-lose, from where we were going for dinner to the choices we were making for our children or our family, where we were going to live, what our budget would be, and more. Everything was a battle. No one died, but we lost. Taking the competitiveness out of the relationship and becoming one has been a crucial factor in making our marriage last.

These win-win lessons also apply to our relationships outside our home. Having everyone involved understand a decision and how choices will benefit everyone results in better teams, workplaces, and relationships.

"When we were first married, our competitive nature turned every argument into a battle to win. It took a few years for us to realize that we weren't really winning at all when we were fighting against each other. Whether I won an argument or he won, we both lost. When we started fighting for each other—fighting for unity instead of being right—we really won. You can't win unless you're winning together." —Lauren Depew

Samantha and Lauren

The world wants you to remain two separate individuals in conflict rather than become one at peace. It says you're responsible for your own happiness and for taking care of your own needs, and of course that's true. The difference is that as a loving spouse, you should also want to do those things for your partner that bring them happiness.

Finding a Friend Instead of a Foe

Becoming one requires putting each other above all the other relationships in our lives and making choices together—not in the battlefield, but in a discussion. These are all things we've learned from the wonderful guidance we've received over the years, whether it was from a friend or a pastor. It did not happen overnight; it was a process. God wants us to be not only of one flesh but also of one mind. A definite factor in our becoming one was putting God in the center of our marriage and knowing that no matter what happens, God has our back. That one thing removed many of our disagreements. **You can tell when our priorities have gotten out of kilter. Our voices get louder, our tempers get shorter, and our peace is replaced with separateness.**

Having people around you who will support your marriage is critical. In the beginning of our marriage, it felt as if we were surrounded by people who would have loved for us to get divorced. They could have us to themselves. The friends we have now are our biggest cheerleaders. In fact, I have one girlfriend who has always lovingly corrected me and held me accountable many times.

> Whenever I would get really frustrated and go to her or just sit there and complain, she would say something like, "You know, Todd's working very hard right now, and he's under a lot of pressure. Yes, that was wrong, but you need to understand where he is."

Having people in your life who love you and have your best interest at heart is an awesome gift. We're really beholden to those people who have been our accountability partners, both personally and professionally.

We both walked into our relationship knowing what we thought marriage was and what we thought we deserved and were entitled to, and we had a really tough time overcoming our preconceptions to come to the right conclusions about marriage. Because we were so locked into what we thought were the "correct" ideas on marriage, we were plagued by a lot of fear and anger. It took us a long time to get past that, get over ourselves, and get to a better place in our marriage.

R-E-S-P-E-C-T

One of the things we argued about constantly was respect. We both wanted to be respected, and we both thought we were respecting each other. We had no idea we had different ideas about what respect really meant. The way Todd wanted to be respected was to be told he was important in my life, that he was doing a great job, and that he was a wonderful husband. And what I wanted was for him to show his respect by doing special things, like taking me out for a nice meal once in a while. Learning our differences and how we each wanted to be shown respect was a crucial part of improving our relationship.

 Tools for Becoming One

Becoming one was a miraculous step in our marriage. It took discipline and courage. More importantly, it took becoming selfless and learning a new language.

Selflessness Samples

- **Put** the toilet seat down.
- **Show** grace when your spouse hurts you.
- **Pick up** the dog poop without announcing it.
- **Serve** your spouse.
- **Be** full of love, even when you have to repeat yourself five times.
- **Apologize**.
- **Give** your spouse the best pancake.
- **Make** decisions together.
- **Sharpen** each other's sword.

> "Marriage is not for the weak! It takes humility and adjustments. Different stages of life take different measures of the same qualities but in different amounts—grace, patience, managing conflicts with win-wins, sacrifice, giving, and receiving." —Amy Smalley

🔅 Learning a New Language

There are so many words. In every relationship and workplace that wants to grow and become extraordinary, what changes is words. To change, we need new ideas and the right language to go with them. What power words have. Words are the way we bring our inner self into the world and make our dreams become reality.

Todd and I had the habit of using destructive words and behaviors for years, so we had to learn new words. We could tear each other apart in the blink of an eye with our unhealthy words. Usually, we cannot get rid of old habits without replacing them with new habits. How we speak is a hard habit to change. Here are some new words that we use habitually now. I hope you find one or two that you like. They are simple and yet powerful.

💗 1. **Be Compassionate**

You **are** an amazing person, and **I have** incredible respect for you.

Thank you for all the ways you **have blessed** my life.

You **are** a wonderful parent.

How **are** you feeling?

What can I **do** for you?

Whatever you **want** to do.

👁 2. **Be Captivating**

I think you **are** the sexiest person on Earth.

What I **like** best about you is …

What **is** important to you?

I **am** proud of you.

Is that **working** for you?

👑 3. **Be Commanding**

I **am** never going to stop loving you, but I do not like you right now.

I **am** going to be on time; you can drive separately if you want.

Will this matter twenty years from now?

This **is** what I want to do.

I **am** too tired to talk about this right now; what time can we talk tomorrow?

It isn't what you **say**; it is your tone of voice.

4. Be Committed

I **want** you.

I **am** sorry for what has happened in past. I **was** wrong. It **will never happen** again.

Yes.

Please only **say** things that honor our marriage.

Let's **watch** a church. (Our church is offered online if we are out of town or obligated, we can watch church.)

5. Be Connected

Thank you for making me a better person.

You **are** my best friend.

I **need** you.

This is what I **heard** you say.

Let's **pray** together.

6. Be Courageous

I **am** sorry that I hurt you; what I **said** wasn't true.

What would you **like** me to change?

I **am** scared.

We cannot **change** the past.

Wow, we **have** a lot to learn.

This **is** really hard for me to talk about.

I **am** a precious artwork of the Lord.

7. Be Creative

One of my favorite times in our marriage **was** when ...

No, you don't **snore**.

Anger **is** an emotion, too.

Let me know when you **have** time to listen.

Would you **like** to be responsible for this?

What **are** possible solutions?

When ridding yourself of bad habits,
plan to replace them with new healthy habits.

MIRACLE: CREATE A CHAMPIONSHIP TEAM

Create a Championship Marriage: Todd and Penni after Big Win

Todd and I both thought getting our degrees would be the pinnacle of our learning, but our marriage remarkably became a place for us to grow, overcome, and learn how to have a relationship. Before we started changing our language, Todd would often say in an argument, "You shouldn't expect our marriage to be perfect. We had Plans A, B, and C (earlier relationships), and since they didn't work, we should expect less from this marriage." That would upset me, and I would bring up everything he had ever done wrong since the beginning of time. Then he would drop the "D" (divorce) word to end the argument. **He never meant it. It was his way of ending the debate and getting to bed.** Thinking back now, I should have been more understanding and empathetic regarding his responsibilities and the pressure he was under.

Dreams Come True!

Many of my girlfriends have said over the years, "I would not want your life." Being a coach's wife is full of challenges, and our marriage has had its bad days, but I would not trade what we have for all the money in the world. I loved Michelle Obama's statement on *The Tonight Show Starring Jimmy Fallon*. "I always say, if you're married for fifty years, and ten of them are horrible, you're doing really good!"[3]

---

[3] Interview on *The Tonight Show with Jimmy Fallon*, December 18, 2018

Today, I see our life as the greatest of adventures. Our passion for each other and the world, our commitment to each other, the memories we share, and the mountains we have climbed together—mentally, emotionally, and spiritually—make for an incredible love story.

I know it is God's Plan A.

Too often, we compare our marriages and lives to others, but comparison can be the death of joy

💡 Create Your Fairy-Tale Marriage

- How is your marriage unique?
- What obstacles have you overcome?
- How does your spouse make you feel special?
- What do you and your spouse share?
- What adventures have you shared?

Create Your Fairy Tale: Todd and Penni at Lady Gaga Concert

👁 Turn Autopilot Off

I find it fascinating that I can live somewhere for years, but one day realize there has been a building a mile from my house that I've never seen. How much of our lives do we spend on autopilot?

What is autopilot? It is the times when we let old habits and others control our lives. When inertia takes over our decision making, our self-awareness is diminished.

Autopilot is especially harmful to a developing a healthy relationship. Todd and I lived on autopilot for years. It was about surviving the challenges and taking the opportunities. We did not take a trip by ourselves until our tenth anniversary. We simply lay on the beach and enjoyed the present. We did not try to solve any problems or plan the future. So much of our lives, we are taught our worth is in what we "do." Being able to spend time together without doing anything made our relationship stronger. We knew our relationship was not based on performance but on mutual love. Living on autopilot not only brings unhappiness and leaves us stuck, it stops us from growing spiritually, physically, mentally, and emotionally.

> "One study says that 90 percent of our everyday behavior is based on our habits. . . . That means how we treat people, how we spend our money, what we watch, what we listen to—90 percent of the time, we're on autopilot. We do what we've always done." —Joel Osteen

Travel is our biggest weapon for turning off autopilot. We actually started leaving the United States because so many people would recognize Todd from television. Our first couple of trips were with Prestonwood Baptist Church. We followed the steps of Paul through Greece, the islands of the eastern Mediterranean, and Ephesus. The next year, we were supposed to go to Israel, but Todd started his first head coaching position at Rice. He was dead set that we were not going. Thankfully, Jack Graham changed Todd's mind. That trip still remains the best adventure! Since then we have added thirty-one countries and only have three states left to visit all fifty! We have incredible memories and beautiful stories we share.

Travel is the best way to get yourself out of autopilot. Seeing new cultures creates new ideas, and visiting new places broadens our view of beauty. Travel reveals how similar we all are and breaks down the walls that separate us. Travel shows us how grateful we need to be for our home and country. Travel pushes us to try new things and do things differently. It is the best development activity!

Learning How to Play with Discipline

On the football field, discipline is essential to win a game. The field itself is organized as a rectangle, 120 yards long and 40 yards wide for a college football field. The ten yards on either end of the field are the scoring zones. This gives football teams 100 yards to travel in either direction to score a touchdown or a field goal. These dimensions never change in college football, so the players must be just as predictable in their skills. The coach is the teacher, both on the field and off, so the player must learn everything possible from the coach's strategy to win the game. Discipline gives the player the ability to achieve the necessary muscle mass in the body through proper eating and weight lifting so that the coach can place the player at the right position on the field. Discipline gives the player the ability to throw the ball to a target, catch the ball, and run with the ball—skills developed and honed during daily practice. Finally, discipline gives the players the ability to focus on scoring as the clock runs down to the last minute—even the last seconds—of a game. The same holds true with all the we strive to do. Almost all couples have the same landscape of challenges: communication, chores, conflicts, and children. If you are disciplined, you can have a championship marriage.

Marriage Advice from Friends, Fans, and Family

Sometimes the best advice is found by listening to multiple voices. With that in mind, I have collected the following marriage advice from friends, fans, and family.

- "Effective communication 24/7/365, along with love and respect are imperative to having a successful marriage." Melissa Cohen
- "Kevin and I have been married for twenty-five years. We make sure to spend time together weekly. We meet for lunch during the week, we plan date nights together, and we vacation together without our children. We also don't go to bed angry." Sherry Brooks
- "Roads leading to marriage are fun and exciting but don't panic when things start to develop rough patches. Just like on a football field, *communication* is the key component to working through every obstacle in life. My wife and I continue to

talk about everything and don't always agree but we *always* find some type of mutual ground and reasoning! Happy wife, happy life!" Justin Shuman

- "Be best friends first. Let yourself be madly, wildly, unabashedly crazy about your spouse. Be real with your spouse, always. Most importantly, make Christ the center of your relationship." Janice Hansen
- "Be quick to say sorry and quicker to forgive." Jeff Higginson
- "Being married for twenty years, marriage is team work; working together makes a huge difference in all the decisions you have to make in life together. But we put God first. When you put God first in your marriage, he helps you see things that need to be worked on and the beauty of working as one together." Tracy Sanders
- "My husband played in the NHL for seventeen years, and the hardest part was he had to miss his kids' milestones: games, school events, etc. He missed a lot; it was his sacrifice for playing a game he loved. *But* my kids and I always knew how special, important, and loved we were by him." Kristen Sullivan
- "Spend the time you need to know each other and to understand what your spouse needs. I prefer time to gifts; my husband benefits from words of affirmation. Everyone is different; learn about each other continually—people do change. Grow and change together, and marriage is a beautiful gift. It's my very favorite thing!" Sheri Alsguth
- "Pick your battles and fight them gently. None of us are perfect, but we can grow to love each other's' imperfections in a way that strengthens our relationships." Victoria Goldwasser
- "Marriage is all about communication and choices. I don't believe in 50/50. I believe in both partners being 100/100. Communication is key in a marriage. You will both grow and change over the years, and it is a choice to keep choosing your partner. Know that storms will come, but if you can love your partner more than you love yourself, you will see the fruit of that eventually. Marriage is this beautiful relationship that changes over time, but at the core of it is a partnership and love that no other relationship can even come close to." Sharon Fulwider
- "It is 100 percent for both spouses. You enter a room with no exits!" Sandy Scheer

TENACIOUS DICIPLINE SUMMARY

Stop the insanity of repeating the same mistakes.

Execute a strategic mindset and organization.

Strive to continuously improve.

Remember "Complexity in organization makes simplicity for operations." —Tom Landry

Knowledge builds confidence and connections.

Perform every minute, every day, as champions.

Reward and celebrate performance.

love unconditionally

Never quit; be blessed!

TENACIOUS
TOUGH

BE A **WARRIOR**
NOT A **WORRIER**

ALL
IN!

PLAYBOOK

THE GRAHAM GAME PLAN

OPPOSITION'S TOUGH STRATEGY

THE TOUGH CALL SHEET: 7 C's

4
Playbook for
TENACIOUS
TOUGH

Go from Fatiguied to Fierce

"Every obstacle is an opportunity to improve one's condition."

—Author Unknown

THE OBSTACLES IN OUR PATH

In ancient times, a king had a boulder placed on a roadway. Then he hid himself and watched to see if anyone would remove the huge rock. Some of the king's wealthiest merchants and courtiers came by and simply walked around it.

Many loudly blamed the king for not keeping the roads clear, but none did anything about getting the big stone out of the way. Then a peasant came along carrying a load of vegetables. On approaching the boulder, the peasant laid down his burden and tried to move the stone to the side of the road. After much pushing and straining, he finally succeeded. As the peasant picked up his load of vegetables, he noticed a purse lying in the road where the boulder had been. The purse contained many gold coins and a note from the king indicating that the gold was for the person who removed the boulder from the roadway. The peasant learned what many others never understand: every obstacle presents an opportunity to improve one's condition.

In this story, the peasant demonstrates mental and physical toughness by facing adversity with a positive attitude, embraces his ability to take on tough assignment, and wants to contribute to his community without reward. Every obstacle is an opportunity to become a Tough Warrior.

THE GRAHAM GAME PLAN FOR TENACIOUS TOUGH

GOAL: Become a Tough Warrior.

RELATIONSHIP: Live with a Heart of Hope.

AGENCY: Practice Practicing.

HABITS: Understand the Myth of Things.

ADVENTURE: Taking Tough Assignments.

MIRACLE: Becoming a Warrior, not a Worrier.

OPPOSITION'S TOUGH STRATEGY

Strain until you are constantly fatigued.

Maintain unclear and unfair expectations.

Perpetuate angry mindset to deplete your energy.

Increase your frustration through frustration.

Behave with mental, emotional, and physical **laziness**.

Ignore advice from experts.

Focus on process, not problems.

Worry about what everyone else wants and thinks.

Run away from challenges.

Live in comfort zone.

TOUGH

THE 7 C's TOUGH CALL SHEET: TAKE ACTION

1. Be Compassionate.
Controlling your autonomic system.

2. Be Captivating.
Remove distractions.

3. Be Commanding.
Make hard choices.

4. Be Committed.
Practice Practicing.
Take tough assignments.

5. Be Connected.
Take away the pacifier.
Find Mentors.

6. Be Courageous.
Remain hopeful during adversity.
Stop doing God's job.
Dance to a different time.

7. Be Creative.
Plan for adversity.
Be a minimalist.

GOAL: BECOME A TOUGH WARRIOR

Tough Mind, Heart, and Spirit

Toughness is a quality we find everywhere in nature. We also find it in civilization. Toughness is also known by other names: durability, hardness, roughness, strength, flexibility, and resilience. Every human needs toughness because of all the creatures in nature, we are the most vulnerable to creatures in the wild and to the elements. A baby is the most vulnerable creature because it lacks toughness. Traditionally, we think we acquire toughness by developing our muscles, eating healthy foods, exercising arms and legs, and developing strong bones. Good nutrition is the essential building block of toughness in every individual. We lack fur and hard flesh, fangs in the mouth, claws on our hands and feet, and adequate muscles to outrun most animals. The only way we can survive is by developing technology to protect us and developing the ability to tolerate pain.

"Mindful Toughness" is a byproduct of tolerating pain, because the human brain releases endorphins to soothe us at the very moment we stretch our muscles beyond their normal range. Humans get a rush of pleasure as these endorphins flood the body, and many people experience euphoria. However, this happens only when the individual exercising can tolerate the pain for a few minutes until the endorphins kick in. If the individual stops exercising to avoid the pain, the brain will not release the endorphins. This is why athletes in every sport and people who exercise in gyms tell us, "No pain, no gain!" If you are not willing to experience a few minutes of pain as you push your muscles beyond their normal range of activity, then you will not experience the intense pleasure of the endorphin rush as your brain attempts to soothe those aching muscles. Once the endorphin rush kicks in, you will get a boost of energy to stretch your muscles even more, because you want to keep feeling good. This boost of energy helps us to continue exercising, continue running, continue playing a game to the very last moment.

Being tough like this means that your body buys into the exercise instead of retreating from it. Your cells switch from screaming, "Stop this pain!" to shouting, "Yes, bring on the pleasure!" Your body is hard-wired by evolution for this switch, so take advantage of it. This is what it means to go *all in*! If you are an athlete playing on a field when that rush of energy hits you, you realize that every cell of your body wants to win, every muscle in your body is yearning for more pleasure after the initial running on the field. Your teammates on the field feel this, and they want more. When football players experience this energy rush during a game, every single player, every single coach, every single fan, and every single relative watching the game is *all in* for victory. Even if the team loses the game, the endorphin rush that pushed the team to play at its best will linger, helping the team train and exercise, giving the players the necessary lift to win the next game. Part of being physically tough is having the tools to manage your body's reaction to stress when you are under pressure. I learned through a year visiting doctors at Mayo Hospital in Scottsdale: **the autonomic nerve system is major contributor to your body's reaction to stress**. I learned three keys to controlling my autonomic nerve system. You can do these anytime, anywhere, and everyone can learn.

 ## Three Keys to Controlling My Autonomic Nerve System

1. *Re-name Your Emotions*—When I felt my heartbeat rising and my body starting to become tense, I would label it anxiety. I named it anxiety, so it was. Then a doctor explained to me that when those symptoms start, I should name it excitement. This remarkably changes the processes in my brain. Instead of these symptoms leading my body's off button, I suddenly felt a smile across my face and a sense of anticipation. Other examples I practice include:

   Fear: New Adventures.

   Frustration: Gratitude for Choices.

   Pressure: Importance of What I am Doing.

   It does take practice and it's important to plan for what your new emotion will be when faced with different kinds of stress.

2. *Just Breathe*—For some reason, when I feel pressure or stress, I tend to hold my breath, basically depriving my brain of oxygen. You can imagine the negative impact. Other people start breathing quickly and erratically when faced with tough situations. There are many breathing techniques that are useful in different situations. Consciously breathing is critical to escape the fear and flight reaction

of your body. Slow and controlled breathing lowers your blood pressure and heart rate and tells your brain, "No need to panic."

3. ***Focus on the Task at Hand.*** Even when I am getting a massage, my mind starts to worry and focus on what might happen later or reflect on a stressful situation from the past. We cannot be in the present if we suffer from distraction. When your mind concentrates on the task at hand, your body will to and improve your performance or circumstance greatly.

⟨ RELATIONSHIP: LIVE WITH A HEART OF HOPE ⟩

The heart of toughness is remaining committed. The fans know this all too well: the true fan is not someone watching the team when it is winning a championship but the person watching the team when it is losing during the regular season. The true fan is there, loyal to the team, when everyone else is busy doing other things. If the fan is committed to the team, the players must be no less committed, because the players are playing for the team, the fans, their friends, their relatives, and the institution. The test of your commitment is how tough you are in playing for the team even after you lose a game. We all get weary at times when faced with loss or adversity. Whether you are weary of relentless work, frustration of outcomes, of always having to be the positive one or just exhausted, it is when you feel like you have nothing left to give. Hope is the answer to weariness. Hopelessness destroys hearts. Hope energizes us when we think our goals are impossible. Hope is what keeps your commitment and the greatest weapon of a heart of toughness.

 Strategies to Remain Hopeful during Adversity

1. ***Laugh.*** I find laughter can put what appeared to be impossible situations in new light and reveal they are not as disastrous as I thought. Avoid negative people, places, and media.
2. ***Remember Mountains.*** Recall the mountains you thought you would never climb, and you did.
3. ***Practice Secret Random Acts of Kindness.*** This makes your heart so happy! It helps the hope inside your heart grow

exponentially. Changes your view of your problems and helps you appreciate your opportunities.

"Spiritual Toughness" is seen in our devotion to God and team. Just as the brain gives the body an endorphin boost, our devotion gives each individual a boost of grace and spiritual energy if the player shows faith on and off the field. We were blessed with incredible spiritual family who taught us so much about love and faith. **The individuals who are most committed also usually end up performing best on the field of life, a life filled with love, peace and joy.** Isn't that interesting! This devotion—to God, loved ones, and the team—simply means the individual on or off the field acquires a rather unique ability: the capacity to love more as he grows in his faith and toughness.

How Love Impacts the Game

People who love people more are easy to spot, especially on the field. They are always praising and supporting each other producing endorphins and the other bonding hormone, oxytocin. When athletes bond together during rigorous training and the game day, they have the capacity to play better than another team that lacks this bonding. They play with intuition and coordination, leading to sometimes miraculous victories at the last second. The more the players love the game and each other, the more likely they will play with fewer mistakes because each player enters "the zone," moving quickly and intuitively to make the best possible plays in the game. **The impact of devotion applies to all organizations and relationships.**

AGENCY: PRACTICE PRACTICING

From this we can see that mental toughness gives you passion because you love more. It gives you a strong work ethic because you cannot wait to train your body every day so that you can experience that endorphin rush, and it helps you embrace the grind of daily exercise and practice. No athlete becomes a top performer without a daily routine of good nutrition, good exercise, and rigorous practice to train for the main event. Malcolm Gladwell popularized the idea of practicing for 10,000 hours to train your brain, your body, and even your spirit in a structured, focused activity. If we divide 10,000 hours by eight hours per day, the result is about three years and six months for any athlete to train to peak performance. **The daily grind of eight hours of practice is something that every individual should look forward to, because this practice lays the foundation for winning games and championships.**

If you want to reach peak performance, you cannot miss a single day of practice. Many people cannot do this by themselves, so they need a coach to keep them accountable to sustain daily practice. Without accountability, many people easily get distracted from their daily routines, developing bad habits instead of good habits. Some of those bad habits even turn into addictions that are hard to break. Accountability is critical for maintaining both physical and mental and spiritual toughness.

The temptation to break a healthy habit or a routine is very strong, so the tough-minded know they must never quit. The body can be weak, but the tough mind can prevent the body from stopping before reaching a goal. This is why mental toughness must come first. Without mental toughness, it becomes too easy to stop whenever the body encounters pain during an exercise routine. The tough individual, the tough athlete, thinks "I am blessed" while sticking to healthy habits. Not only does the brain reward the body with endorphins for sticking with it, but God rewards the believer for reaching their full potential.

The tough mind is a byproduct of good planning. We all know what good planning looks like: it requires a "what" and a "when." An athlete with a tough mind knows how to depend on the coach for a good plan on the field. The athlete with a tough mind knows how to depend on plans created by the coach for personal training in the gym. A good plan takes account of adversity. If a good plan combines "what" and "when," then the plan must adapt whenever the "what" or the "when" changes. Life happens, so the good athlete who is mentally tough makes contingency plans with the coach to plan for adversity.

> As the Chinese General Sun Tzu notes, "Victorious warriors win first and then go to war, while defeated warriors go to war first and then seek to win."[1]
>
> Richard Heckler tell us that "The path of the Warrior is lifelong, and mastery is often simply staying on the path."[2]

Riding the Bus: Prepare for Adversity

One of the perks of college football is traveling with your football family on road trips. Chartering an entire aircraft and being escorted on luxury tour buses is something you can definitely get used to when compared to everyday travel. Several people have seen the team's grand entrance on television before the kick-off when the broadcast shows the team getting off the bus and heading into the stadium for pre-game activities. What they don't show is the police escort, which is typically involved throughout the length of the trip. This is especially true when you spend an entire week at a bowl site. On these trips, you are able to build relationships with these police officers, who typically support your team going into game day. At times, our police escorts during bowl week have displayed support for our teams by placing our decals on their motorcycle helmets. We have been fortunate to have been taken care of by some of the best men from across the country. Unfortunately, it doesn't always turn out perfectly, as these police officers put their lives at risk by blocking traffic and paving the way for the team buses (typically caravans with three or more buses) to stay on schedule.

While we were at Rice in 2006, we traveled to Orlando, Florida, to play University of Central Florida, and that particular police escort was an experience we will never forget. In the caravan, the head coach, the starters, and priority personnel typically travel on the first bus and most of the support staff members, coaches' families, and administrators all travel in the back (the third or fourth bus). As our Rice football team left the World Marriott and headed to the Citrus Bowl for kick-off, we were escorted by a team of motorcycle

---

[1]   Tzu, Sun. *The Art of War.* 500 BC
[2]   Heckler, Richard Strozzi. *In Search of the Warrior Spirit: Teaching Awareness Disciplines to the Green Berets.* Berkeley: North Atlantic Books, 1990, 1992, 2003

officers. When the caravan has to cross a busy intersection, these police officers position themselves to block traffic and override the streetlights so that the buses can pass. As we exited the Marriott, however, one distracted driver in a small red Ford truck did not stop for the police blockade and charged through the first four-way intersection, crashing into the first bus, which had all of our priority personnel on board, including Todd, who was sitting in the first row. I was on bus three in the front seat and watched the tragedy. I was so concerned about the driver, but also thought of injuries our players and coaches might have received due to the collision. The truck had not attempted to slow down at all and had collided with the right side of our bus at around fifty miles per hour.

Two seconds most likely saved the motorcycle officer's life, who was inches from being struck by the truck. This accident totaled the bus, which could not be driven and had to be left smoking on the side of the street. The Ford truck took the majority of the damage, getting trapped underneath the bus. The passenger in the truck also was severely injured. This created a chaotic scene on the side of the road as the players and coaches in the first bus were in shock.

Fortunately, our team doctors located in the back of the third bus were able to provide some assistance to this struggling driver and the passengers on the first bus as help was quickly called to the scene. If our doctors had not been there, the driver most likely would have lost his life. As you can imagine, Todd was initially worried about everyone's safety. But as soon as everyone was cleared by the doctors, the team and coaches boarded the third bus and headed to the stadium with police escort. Needless to say, the team had been through so much. It takes mental toughness to maintain the focus and fortitude necessary to secure a victory. Todd, his coaches, and the leadership on the team were quick to reset their minds and get our team back on track.

Our team responded and came together in all three phases, playing disciplined and mistake-free football for four quarters to beat the Golden Knights 40–29. Looking back, nothing came easy for the 2006 Rice Owls football team. The team had a unique ability to thrive in adverse situations, and this was just one of many times when they proved they were built differently.

💡 Plan for Adversity

- **Expect** the unexpected and plan for worst-case scenarios.
- **Know** that you are not in control of everything, so have back-up plans when your first plan does not work out.
- **Keep** the intended purpose in your mind. Adapt to unexpected situations to achieve your intended purpose.
- **Control** your reactions to unexpected events: it's fine to get upset or angry for a brief moment, but always return to a calm mood.
- **Look** for the silver lining every time. Every bad experience has a silver lining.

Todd has been a warrior from the start. His sister tells this story about how Todd reacted to his father leaving his family.

When I was twelve and Todd was fourteen, our father brought us a letter with a hundred dollars in it, stating he was leaving and wouldn't be back. He said one day we'd understand. I remember my brother watching me read it and tears running down my face. I heard how angry he was. He told me, "Don't worry, Sheree. I'll show Daddy what he left behind." Times were so hard. Mom worked three jobs to take care of us. Our air-conditioner went out in the summer of 1982. That was one of the hottest summers ever. People were frying eggs on the sidewalk in downtown Dallas. I'll never forget that heat. My mom's friend loaned mom the money to get us a window unit and her husband put it in. We struggled so much, but I didn't realize how bad things were because mom always somehow got us the things we needed. We had something money couldn't buy: love. We all loved each other, and we loved being together. I think those hard times were some of the best days in my life because I had brothers who loved me and would do anything for me, so losing my father wasn't as hard.

To those who use well what they are given, even more will be given. (Matthew 25:29)

HABIT: UNDERSTAND THE MYTH OF THINGS

We both were born on the tough side of Dallas. Todd shared a room with his three brothers. He could always tell from week to week whether there was any money by what his mom served for dinner. In the good weeks, there was meat in the spaghetti; in the bad weeks, there was just sauce, no meat. Their barber was their mom, and their clothes were hand-me-downs. After his dad left them, they struggled to pay the bills, and it was hard to put food on the table for the family.

Todd's mom Carol had an eighth-grade education and worked three jobs to keep the family in the same small home in Mesquite they had lived in since the children's births. By the age of eleven, we had both started working. I babysat neighborhood kids on a regular basis. Todd passed out circulars around neighborhoods and helped his brothers deliver newspapers. He started bagging groceries at the Skaggs-Alpha Beta when he was fifteen years old. At fifteen, I was serving breakfast at The Little Chef on weekends and hosting at Figaro's Pizza in the evenings. We both learned a strong work ethic at a very young age.

When I was born, my mom lived in a little single-wide mobile home near the Love Field airport. As a single mom off and on for many years, my mom didn't make much money. We were not impoverished, but we lived with very modest means. For various reasons—usually related to marriage, divorce, or money—we moved many times during my childhood, living in apartments most of the time. I grew up on mac and cheese, bologna, Spam, and peanut butter and honey sandwiches (which I still think are awesome!). By the time I was nine, we moved into a home and lived in a middle-class neighborhood. I felt like a princess. However, this financial stability did not last for long.

Even though we lived in modest circumstances, **Todd and I have great memories that fill our senses, like long, hot days spent outside, unsupervised, and not having to be home until the street lights came on.** Even though we were not rich and faced times of real financial struggle, we never thought we did without. We never feared going without a meal or a place to live and are grateful for our family and friends who loved us. **It is truly relationships that make a life.**

Our beginnings were small in many ways; we had no idea how drastically our lives would change. Our background

helped us become risk takers and fearless when necessary. **These qualities gave us the capacity to do more and be more with less.** Our lives were not based on the money in our back accounts or the things in our house. I bought most of my clothes and furniture at secondhand shops. I still frequent them. After moving thousands of miles multiple times, I gave up my hoarding habits and Todd stopped putting photos in the corners of framed art and randomly on furniture. Now when we move, everything that does not have a place is left in the front yard and donated or taken to consignment.

What I learned from having nothing and almost anything: Things create stress. Things require management, care, space, money, and responsibility, so instead of living life, you spend time taking care of stuff. God's purpose for your life is not about things. Do not get caught up in worldly ideas of success, as we did at moments. Success isn't what you have. In fact, what you have may prevent you from the true moments of happiness and gifts of the present, because you are so concerned about keeping things or earning more to take care of things. Do not let things block your path to success.

Dakota, our second youngest, is a minimalist. I strive to learn from him. What a great way to live!

How to be a Minimalist, Photo of Dakota

 **How to Be a Minimalist**

Consider these questions to learn how to be a minimalist.

- Do you need and use everything in your house?
- Do you have a large wardrobe? Do you need everything in your closet?
- Do you eat too much? Can you live well by eating less?
- Do you live in a big house or a small apartment? Would your life improve by living in a smaller space?
- How much money can you save every month? Are you able to save more than you are saving now?
- What things are taking away your time, space, and money? What can you donate, sell, or give away?

ADVENTURE: TAKING TOUGH ASSIGNMENTS

Through toughness, Todd and I rapidly moved up the ladder of success. I was twenty-six when I graduated with a degree in historical philosophy. Everyone told me there was no way I would ever get a teaching job, because in Texas, coaches taught most history courses, and I was not a coach. But when I went on my first and only job interview, the principal hired me. He must have seen something special in me I did not know yet.

After my first semester of teaching, he put me in charge of staff development for the whole school, teaching teachers about how to motivate their students. By the next year, I was head of the History Department, and I had a student teacher under me. Of course, there was a lot of jealousy and drama that came with the job because the other teachers had been there for years, and the youngest of them was ten years my senior.

Dealing with success is not always easy. I cried driving home every day, because I wanted people to like me! I look back and giggle now. While I was home that summer, I rewrote the curriculum. I eliminated objectives that weren't helpful to our 99 percent free-lunch population, whose first language was not English. They needed to know where they were, not who the famous jazz singer from east Texas was. I also made everything project-based, so they would be active and learn new skills.

I presented it to the teachers when we arrived back at school for staff development. **Instead of the gratitude I thought it would receive, they went into rebellion.** They were going to be using the lesson plans they had for a decade, including worksheets and tests. Of course, there were so many ways I failed here. **But the experience prepared me for great adventures later on. I learned that everyone has their own rate of adapting to change.** Some of us are anxious to find new solutions to problems, while others think: if it's not broken, do not fix it. I learned that change is not easy for everyone. I also learned that other people's feelings are not my responsibility, but as a leader, I need to know and adapt to my team's needs. I started seeing people by their reaction to change. There are agents, adapters, accepters, and avoiders. **Accepting and adapting to others' personality types builds better relationships and teams.**

Penni and Dr. Barbara Erwin

The first school I taught at my first two years was like driving a stock car compared to the rocket ship I boarded in 1994. Dr. Barbara Erwin had a great impact on both Todd and me. Dr. Erwin was our superintendent when Todd and I worked in the Allen School District. She always pushed us to become our best as educators and leaders by providing constant development for us. **She had really high expectations and wanted us to be the absolute best at everything we were doing, whether it was on the football field or in the classroom.**

What happened to my career in the following years was more like a rocket ship. In 1994, I opened Curtis Middle School (Allen, TX) as the teacher for the gifted and talented. **Every day in the classroom was an adventure, and I felt like I was in heaven.** I loved everything about it. One day, my principal, Ted Moore, approached me about an opportunity to be part of a new technology that was being introduced. It was called the Internet. Lance Boxer, who was the CIO of MCI, had a son in my class. I had no idea what the Internet was and never had any technological training. My first time on the Internet, I stayed up for twenty-four hours straight after the modem connection, which took seven minutes. I found an ability I didn't know I had. I fluently spoke HTML and understood random systems. As far as I know, my middle school students were the first in country to produce their own web pages in 1995.

By 1996, I had my own staff on each campus, and we created the first virtual high school. I spoke to the Texas State Senate about the future of education. I started speaking nationally and internationally about how the Internet could change education from bricks and mortar, and how we could customize education for students with this new tool. In 1996, we held the first webpage competition. Vint Cerf, one of the true inventors of the Internet, was our judge! It was like constantly living in the future, my dream—which is my gift and my curse.

I moved up the educational ladder and ran out of room, so I moved to the corporate world in 1999 and, for the first time, had a six-figure job and an important title. **However, I missed the long hours and excitement of tackling tough tasks. When you are doing an important task, your job title does not matter.** You feel a great sense of importance and satisfaction. I had spent the previous nine years drastically changing classrooms and schools, and we had even written grants for over ten million dollars from the US Department of Education to spread our wealth of knowledge and technology across the state. I had won national awards and received international recognition for leadership. I had graduated from college only eight years earlier.

Todd's career path was a similar rocket ride. He started as a ninth-grade history and health teacher, in addition to being a seventh and eighth grade football coach. He went from being an educator and middle school assistant football coach at age 24 to being a defensive coordinator at a small college by the time he was 26. In 1993 the East Central Tigers (Todd's alma mater) won the NAIA National Championship, playing against none other than Rich Rodriguez, the other team's head coach and offensive coordinator, for the first time. Rich produced the number one offense in the country in NAIA and Todd fielded the nation's number one defense. Seven years later, Rich gave Todd his first Division 1 college football job at West Virginia University. By the time he was twenty-eight, Todd was a high school head coach. He was also athletic director, so he was responsible for all the other coaches of volleyball, basketball, softball, baseball, soccer, etc. By the time he was thirty-six, he was a defensive coordinator for a D-1 college football program, and at the age of forty-one, he became a D-1 head football coach at Rice University.

He went from someone who wasn't even expected to go to college to becoming not just a coach, but the head coach of the prestigious NCAA D-1 university. He was named Coach of the Year three times.

We were blessed with a career track that was unique because we did not want to put ourselves in a box. **We said "yes" to a lot of things that other people did not. We seemed to gravitate to the tough tasks.** We could always figure it out. There were probably hundreds of people more qualified to take on the Internet project, but I think I was selected because of my work ethic, passion, and love of learning.

When Todd moved from Oklahoma to take head coaching job at Allen High School in 1995, they had not won a district game in three years. Many people turned down the Allen job before Todd took it. If he had not taken that job, we would never have met. By 1996, they were Bi-District champions and in 1998 the team flew to Odessa Permian and beat opponents at Ratliff Stadium (made famous in *Friday Night Lights*). Now, Allen High School football is known as a national power with many state championships and a 60-million-dollar stadium that mesmerizes everyone. **The word "overachiever" has always driven me crazy, as an educator and individual. Todd and I did not overachieve. We were warriors. We took on tough tasks with passion, purpose, and perseverance.**

Todd and Penni in Allen

Pat Riley summarizes the true warrior's attitude:

"The true Warrior understands and seizes that moment by giving an effort so intense and so intuitive that it could only be called one from the heart." [3]

Hard Choices and Hard Work

Todd has demonstrated his abilities as a warrior by coaching college football under many difficult conditions. One of the hardest things to do when making tough decisions is not to decide rashly but to make sure you really let your values and your principles guide you. Over the years, we've made some good decisions, some bad ones, and a few ugly ones. The bad and ugly decisions have been the exception. For the most part, we have let our principles and values guide us.

When making tough decisions, we reflect on who we are. Our faith, character, discipline, and toughness are rooted in the values we

---

[3]   Riley, Pat. *The Winner Within*, Berkeley, 1994

stand for. **It is so important to not compromise our values. The biggest thing to remember is that making tough decisions is part of the job of leadership.** The key to making great decisions is to have a process in place so that you don't make decisions based solely on emotions. **Most of the mistakes we've made have come about because we let our emotions get in the way.**

Todd's greatest asset is his passion. There were times at Tulsa when he worked so hard, he slept in the office. There were times he missed our kids' events. He regrets missing those events, but he knew he wanted to be good to his staff and make sure that they didn't miss *their* kids' events. However, as a coach he sometimes could not follow his own values because his team was on the road or playing a game. This is hard for others to understand.

There have been times when he looked back and knew he had made bad calls. There have been times when he has given students extra chances. He loves kids and is always going to err on the side of giving guys another chance and helping them, but without lowering his program's standards for anyone.

It's ugly anytime you lose to your rival, as we did when we lost two games to Arizona. We also were fortunate to have beaten them four times, making Todd the only coach in ASU history to be undefeated at home during the Territorial Cup. Losing to Arizona was just unbearable. At Tulsa, we hated losing to Houston. We had some epic battles with our rivals, and most of the time we were victorious, but that's what college football is all about.

Sometimes he made the wrong decision about a recruit. Sometimes he brought a talented young man to a school, but the athlete did not fit the culture or the program. Those are the toughest times for Todd, because he takes 100 percent responsibility for all his decisions. When it comes to drug testing, it's all about being proactive instead of being reactive.

Todd has taught young men how to live championship lives, including how to be a championship husband, father, son, brother, and loyal friend. He teaches men that life is about relationships: the good , the bad, and the ugly times come along with it. **That's what makes relationships: the adversity and the tough times you go through, when you get knocked down and get back up.** Your teammates, your family, and the people who love you and help pull you back up. That's what it means to be part of a team, part of a family.

 **Making Hard Choices**

- **Make** a decision with time, not on a whim or because of your mood at a specific moment.
- **Have** a process of two to three steps to take before making an important decision.
- **Ask** other people for their input before making a big decision.
- **Think** of all the possible consequences, both negative and positive.
- **Stop** blaming other people for bad decisions. You are the person who made the decision.

People Pleasers Are Pacifiers

Football recognizes certain boundaries that define who is responsible for what and has an established chain of command. A team plays well when every person focuses only on their specialized task that helps with the game. A player is not a coach, so every player must let the coach do his job. The coach knows strategy, while the player knows the fundamental tactics. This is nearly identical to the division in the army between the general, the captain, and the soldiers: the general knows the strategy, the captain gets the order to implement the strategy, and the soldier follows the order, using the battlefield tactics learned during training. Similarly, on the football field, the quarterback is the captain implementing the strategy set by the coach. Each player has the task of performing his specialized role. If people start stepping outside of their boundaries, it is more difficult to win a game. Imagine if the tight end told the offensive linemen, "I'll take care of the defense line for this play." He can stay on the bench. **People pleasers do something like this daily. People pleasers are killing the team and themselves.**

As the number of people in our lives grew, my desire to please everyone also grew. Anyone who is a people pleaser knows you always place other people's needs ahead of your own, to the point where your own needs become invisible, even to you, because you think having your own needs makes you selfish. As people pleasers, I felt a constant internal battle. **As Todd's coaching career advanced, not only did I put his career before mine, I put his needs before mine, our kids' needs before mine, friends' needs before mine, fans' needs before mine, and donors' needs before mine. Anyone observing me at the time probably thought all of these relationships gave me a fun and fearless life. Instead, I experienced the exact opposite: anxiety, fear, shame, and guilt.**

> *Money doesn't talk, it swears. Bob Dylan[4]*

The anxiety came first because, as more people came into our lives, I thought I had the responsibility to please them. I felt shame and guilt as I started wanting to take care of my own needs first. God took me down physically a couple of times to prove life would go on without me. Having a huge family to love was an incredible gift that brought us tremendous joy. Yet we were caught in the delicate and complicated effort of balancing time, money, and energy. We simply couldn't make everyone happy.

> *As Irma Kurtz so wisely reminds us, "Givers need to set limits because takers rarely do."*

You can please some of the people all of the time; all of the people some of the time, and some of the people *none* of the time. These are the people you *pray* for *all* of the time. The increased desire to please God and seek *his* approval will decrease the desire to seek approval from others, which will always leave you empty. Always trying to please others is definitely a sure path to stress and failure in life. **Admittedly, as a recovering people pleaser, I can now see how selfish people pleasing is. People pleasers lack the character, discipline, and toughness to accept and respect themselves and others and to live authentic lives.** They act as pacifiers for those they enable.

[4] Dylan, Bob. "It's Alright, Ma (I'm Only Bleeding), *Bringing It All Back Home*, Warner Bros, Inc., 1965

 **Take the Pacifier Away**

1. Ask them to wait.
2. Learn to say *"no."* Practice it, and you do not need any explanations or excuses. You have a choice.
3. Use repetition or walk away. If you are dealing with manipulators, they might not take "no" for an answer. They might even cry or call you names. Just repeat in your mind or aloud, "no," or just walk away.
4. Tell them you have other responsibilities and priorities at this time.
5. Tell them they are capable of doing without it.

Unforeseen Consequences of Success

We faced financial problems from the beginning of our marriage for a simple reason: Our people pleasing and Todd's football coaching career required us to move multiple times, but universities do not pay for football coaches and their families to move, so we had to go into debt just to move. We moved ten times in eleven years. We often found temporary housing, such as the two-bedroom apartment where we lived with our large family and dogs until we could find a house. With some of our moves, we borrowed from my dad so we could move into our new home as we waited to sell the previous house. As we went into debt with each move, Todd and I did the sensible thing by going through consumer credit counseling.

But our financial problems did not disappear as Todd's career rapidly advanced. Instead of eliminating our debt, we went into more debt. This happened because everyone we knew discovered we were suddenly making a lot more money, so friends, relatives, fans, and even complete strangers started asking us for money. We had never before said no to requests for money, and this habit was hard to break, due to our people pleasing problem. Since Todd and I both came from such modest backgrounds, we had no idea how to handle money, and we had difficulty telling people "no." We had been where they were!

We learned there is another name for this problem because so many people have it when they get their first big paycheck: "Sudden Wealth Syndrome." In 2009, *Sports Illustrated* found that 78 percent of NFL players are filing for bankruptcy after only two years of retirement. Sudden Wealth Syndrome causes a psychological desire in these players to make big purchases to prove to themselves that they have made it. This syndrome creates a dangerous and overwhelming feeling that causes athletes to overspend but underthink, resulting in poor financial decisions. At first, having a lot of money was a huge challenge for both of us. Todd was a coach at a public university, so his salary was front-page news. It was like winning the lottery.

We had seen many football athletes go through Sudden Wealth Syndrome, but we didn't recognize it in ourselves. For the first time in our lives, we were not living paycheck to paycheck. **We wanted to share our sudden wealth and say "yes" to everyone.**

However, even though we had more money than ever before, we also had more problems than ever before. We completely enjoyed the act of giving money to people and organizations until we realized it is possible to split a pie in only so many ways. We were so excited to take our friends and relatives on the vacations of their dreams, to put our kids through college, to buy cars for our kids and parents, to give to the charities we love, to tithe to our church, and to help people financially. However, we spent so much money so rapidly that we ended up with more debt. **Consequently, despite having more income, we had also had more stress and strain.**

The same syndrome happens with success on the field and fame. Your team starts experiencing success and gaining attention, so the demand for the coaches' and players' time off the field goes up exponentially. You lose sight of your goals and values and are distracted by outside forces. When you go to your first championship game or bowl game, you want to go to every interview and event. You want your team to have an incredible time. After a great, successful season, you want everyone to have a blast and spend time with their families, friends, and fans, losing focus on success on field on gameday. You lose sight of what caused the wins. You take for granted the time and energy put into each game plan and practice. **Coaches and teams learn this valuable lesson after being embarrassed at their first bowl game.** You are there to win a football game. Your job is to stay focused in the midst of enormous distractions. **Warriors win wars by limiting distractions.**

As Cam Newton said in a press conference, "When you face adversity, that's when you start turning over every rock, stone, pan, and pot just trying to find a way. But when you're winning and you're succeeding, a lot of things get brushed up under the rug, and over time you see a big pile under the rug. At the end of the day, we just have to make sure that we're doing everything that has got us to this point and still focusing in on understanding what our job and our responsibilities are."

 **Warrior Ways to Destroy Distractions**

- **Set up** your day the night before.
- **Have** a positive morning routine.
- **Eliminate** negative people—"Ain't it awfuls" can be time wasters.
- **Close** the door.
- **Be honest and transparent**; people do not ask if they already know.
- **Unplug** media.
- **Care less** what other people think.
- **Prioritize** Important over Urgent—Schedule what is important and do not let urgent interfere.
- **Touch** a piece of paper one time—stop making piles.
- **Have** planned responses and strategies to request.

MIRACLE: BECOMING A WARRIOR, NOT A WORRIER

Stop Doing God's Job

How do you remove the distraction of the money monster? Money monsters can come in many forms. To remove the distraction of our money monster required that we become strategic in our giving. By doing sufficient research, we learned the long-term impact of giving.

We learned that giving money can prevent people from trusting God to take care of them. When you are trying to care for everyone, you're trying to do God's job! When we recognized that we are not God, we stopped feeling the ugliness of guilt and resentment that comes with not being able to please everyone. Trust became a new part of our mindset. Entitlement and jealousy are hard on the soul. But taking care of people when they can take care of themselves only hurts them. As the proverb says, when you give a man a fish, he's going to expect another fish the next day. **There is great joy in giving, but you can hurt yourself and other people by giving in the wrong way at the wrong time.**

Before we learned our lessons, all of this negatively impacted our marriage and our relationships. Now, when I am experiencing stress, anxiety, or frustration in life, I find it is sometimes because I am trying to do God's job. I am not trusting God to fight His battles. **These battles are not mine to fight, but I certainly have wasted lots of time, energy, and money trying.**

Becoming Stewards

On the bright side, even though being millionaires was never on our bucket list, we wanted to make a positive impact on the world, and money helped us do that. Having money taught us many positive lessons. To deal with the money monsters in our life, we sought wisdom from financial experts, including tax attorneys, people who had wealth, and our pastors. We learned that the road to mastering money monsters is paved with good planning. We needed a long-term plan we could reference when anyone asked us for money. **The road map took emotional pressure off both of us: *we* did not say "no" to people; the *road map* said "no" to people.** Like most people who drive to a destination, we did not always follow the map. Sometimes we took detours by giving money to people. But, over time, there were fewer detours.

Seek Sage Advice

Our friend Jack Furst gave us a great formula for being good stewards of our money: spend one-third, save one-third, and give away one-third. This formula has helped us save enough for retirement, put five kids through college, own our home, take fabulous vacations, tithe, give to a variety of causes, and bless our friends and family with gifts.

> We also learned a powerful lesson from Bill Scheer, our pastor at GUTS church in Tulsa. He reminded us of Matthew 6:24: "No one can serve two masters. Either you will hate one and love the other, or you will be devoted to the one and despise the other. You cannot serve both God and money." This verse helped us realize that the money Todd earned from coaching college football is not our money to spend. God has made us stewards of the money. Once we understood this lesson, we changed how we did everything with the money.

As part of this change, we developed a specific strategy to regain our financial health. First, we paid off every loan we had to fulfill Romans 13:8: "Let no debt remain outstanding except the continuing debt to love one another, for whoever loves others has fulfilled the law."

Second, we took to heart Mark 4:19, "The worries of this life, the deceitfulness of wealth and the desires for other things come in and choke the word, making it unfruitful." We realized we could not continue to let money be a monster. As financial expert and radio show host Dave Ramsey says, "You must gain control over your money, or the lack of it will forever control you."[5] We stopped thinking of money as a huge monster trying to destroy us. Instead, we learned to treat money as a resource to be managed.

We are now well equipped to handle money. We are stable financially and we can live a nice, healthy lifestyle. We have learned from experience that it is better to give people experiences instead of money. We have taken great joy in putting our kids through college, which is a legacy we treasure. Mentors gave us many maps to a variety of successes in our lives. We are blessed with some of the best. Our pastors were invaluable in our finding the right paths and many more. Many do not understand the role and goal of mentors. Here are some guidelines to help you find mentors that might give you map for your personal and professional growth.

 **Finding Mentors**

- Mentors are all around us—parents, teachers, coaches. Who are the mentors in your life?
- Be venue specific. Don't look for a financial mentor at a bankruptcy law firm. Look for people with the skills you want to acquire.
- A mentor is someone who can notice your weak areas and coach you. A mentor is not a drinking buddy or acquaintance.
- The best mentors have already experienced what you want to experience. Avoid mentors who have never practiced in your area of need.
- A good mentor is patient and kind. Avoid mentors who are impatient and overly critical.

---

[5]   Ramsey, Dave. *Financial Peace Revisited*, New York: Viking, 2003

Championship Warriors! Those who fought with us and for our teams.

Trusting God's Timing

Change doesn't come without a price.

Early in his professional football career, Todd was cut from the NFL. He was devastated. He had thought the NFL would be his career. He doubted God and was angry. Today, he can see God's wisdom in leading him down a different road, one much more positive than the life he was living as an NFL player.

A couple of times Todd was offered jobs we thought were great opportunities for us, but he didn't get them. Looking back, we can see what a blessing that was, because they both ended up being very poor situations. **We learned to trust that God knows the beginning from the end, and that his timing is perfect. That was another tough one for me, because I'm not a patient person.**

Todd and I dated forever, and it was a difficult dating relationship because we had both had failed marriages. Again, we looked back later and could see God's hand in it all. We both had to grow up. If we had married when we first started dating, before we went through some difficult learning situations, it could have been a total failure.

Three months after we married, Todd took a coaching job in West Virginia—without discussing it with me. I had to make a choice. It caused a custody dispute for my kids, the loss of a high-paying job, my career and another graduate degree, and strong community I enjoyed. I was appalled Todd expected me to just get up and move to West Virginia. We moved to a new environment in West Virginia where we knew no one, and it definitely made us grow together as a couple. Although I did not agree with God's timing, I could see the reasoning in it.

When I think of God's timing, I think of the song, "The Dance," the chorus of which says, "Our lives are better left to chance. I could have missed the pain. But I'd have had to miss the dance."[6]

 What Have I Learned About God's Dance

- God **does** things gradually over time to teach us patience.
- God **sees** the whole picture.
- God **wants** us to measure our lives by love, not time and things.

---

[6] Brooks, Garth. "The Dance" written by Tony Arata, *Garth Brooks*, Capitol Nashville, 1989

Our most recent situation, of course, was when Todd was fired from his position as head football coach at Arizona State University. It was just after a season when the ASU team beat the number-five team in the nation and had exceeded every expectation for the team. They had just won the Territorial Cup for the sixth time in seven years, and Todd was the third-winningest coach in ASU's history. The administration just decided to go a different direction. **Of course, it was both devastating and heartbreaking, because we had put our hearts and souls into creating a legacy there;** we thought we would be at ASU forever. We had just raised a lot of money for a beautiful new building, **but the most important thing was that we had built a lot of incredible relationships.** And then we were gone—overnight. It was very sad.

Everyone we ran into told us they didn't understand why it had happened. It felt like we were asked a thousand times a day, "What are you going to do now?" We almost became hermits, because it was so hard to go out in public. Our response was always, "We were blessed." And we were! Todd held a press conference the day he was dismissed, and he said over and over again how blessed he was to have the opportunity to coach at ASU and how blessed our family had been to have been part of the football program there, especially because of the wonderful relationships we had established.

For us, it was never about the money. We wanted to make a difference, and we felt in that environment we were making a huge difference: with our players, the staff, our fans, and our donors—with everyone. Todd had made an incredibly positive impact on the team. After we left, the school published an article about Todd that read, in part, "He had a plan to infuse the program with a culture that was about winning in all facets of a student-athlete's life. Graham referred to it simply as 'The Sun Devil way.'"[7] The article went on with accolade after accolade about his accomplishments in the school's football program, including raising the team's GPA to over 3.0 for the first time in the program's history. His tenure also had the highest graduation rate in the history of the football program.

So, yes, there was heartbreak associated with his termination. Since then, though, Todd has been able to really enjoy another part of life for the first time. He's spending more time with Michael,

---

[7] https://thesundevils.com/coaches.aspx?rc=673&path=football

who at the age of sixteen needs his dad more than ever. We've been able to spend more time together and do things we've never been able to do, and our relationship is even closer than before. We've traveled to more countries this year than we ever have. Todd has had the opportunity to become a great husband, a great father, and a spiritual leader on a daily basis, which he says is the greatest blessing he's ever had. So even though at the time we were asking, "Why, God?" there was a great reason. I'm seeing that in this season of our life we're having an eternal impact on many people.

My life certainly has been changed, because I was in charge of running everything at home. His job 24/7 was football—period— and everything else was my responsibility. And since I'm half introvert, I need time for solitude; with Todd at home more, I've had to find the time and space for that. We've really had to rely on God, especially in the months right after Todd's termination, to get us through all the changes.

Bob Beaudine and Penni

MIRACLE: BECOMING A WARRIOR, NOT A WORRIER • **187**

In the spring of 2016, before Todd's last season as head football coach at ASU, our great friend Bob Beaudine sent us his amazing book, *2 Chairs*. This book transformed our spiritual life by giving us a simple structure and discipline to communicate and become more intimate with our God. This spiritual growth prepared us for the days ahead when we would lose the job that we loved so much.

Does God know your situation? *Yes!*
Is it too hard for him to handle? *No!*
Does he have a good plan for me? YES![8]

We learned to totally surrender to the Lord and accept completely that he is sovereign. By disciplining ourselves daily during our quiet time with God, we learned to truly listen to God first. We had always read the Word and then prayed and would feel God speak to us. We truly matured as Christians unlike any time in our lives.

Todd's faith has grown exponentially during this time, because he's spent time with God each morning, reading his Bible and asking for direction and discernment. We're grateful for that and for the number of people he's been able to influence. Several of our friends and family have been sick or passed away during the past two years, and he's had the time to be there for them—to be the hands of God in moments when they needed it the most. He believes that has been one of the most valuable things he could be doing with his life. Those memories will stay with him much longer than a football game.

More than anything else, we want our lives to be a testament to God, because without him we definitely would not be where we are now—God-centered in all aspects of our life. And, thankfully, the biggest epiphany we've had has been the peace we've experienced through everything that's happened. We're blessed. **Seeing the worst of times has brought about the best of times.**

[8] Beaudine, Bob. *2 Chairs: The Secret That Changes Everything.* Franklin. TN: Worthy Books, 2018

TENACIOUS TOUGH SUMMARY

- **Be** a warrior, not a worrier.
- *All in*!
- **Love** unconditionally.
- **Be** mentally tough.
- **Work** passionately.
- **Work** ethically.
- **Embrace** the grind.
- **Plan** for adversity.
- **Be** accountable.
- **Never** quit; be blessed!

AFTERWORD

Do You Want to Shrink or Grow?

Tenacious was not meant to be novel. Instead, it tells our stories and says what we learned from the people, places, and programs in our lives. It is full of reflections and tools we apply to help us in our Tenacious journey. It is a way to strengthen the foundations of your life, change your legacy, and become a champion in all aspect of your life:

- Going from **Fruitless to Formidable**
- Going from **Foolish to Foresight**
- Going from **Fractious to Phenomenal**
- Going from **Fatigued to Fierce**

Tenacious **is meant to help you skip personal and professional pain and avoid the mistakes most of us make out of ignorance and shortsightedness.** It also includes descriptions of the ropes we used to climb formidable mountains we faced and conquered. My hope is a story or question made you think in a new way or inspired you to be passionate about your future.

WHAT TO DO NOW?

In the first chapter of *Tenacious*, I encouraged you to come back to the core values exercise on pages 6–8 when you finished reading *Tenacious*. Make time to create core values based on what you want your life to become, using the core value exercise.

1. **Write your new core values** on your bathroom mirror with a dry-erase marker, so you can be reminded each morning and evening how you make choices, behave, feel, and lead.

2. **Reflect on the 7 C's.** How are you going to take action? What do your core values sound, look, act, and feel like?

3. **Create goals based on your reflections**, then use the GRAHAM Plan to give you a structure to live your best life.

Core values determine your actions, and your actions create the goals for your plan. Your plan describes how you will live every year, every day, every moment. The Graham Way!

Living tenaciously means always pushing yourself to be champions on every field of your life. As every football player knows, no one cares about your last game. It is about what you are doing right to become a champion.

You are growing or shrinking!

PHOTOS: FANS, FRIENDS AND FAMILY • **203**

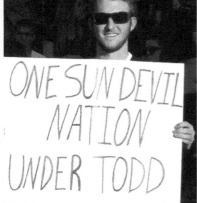

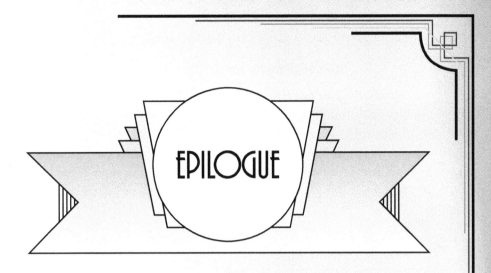

EPILOGUE

It is not the critic who counts; not the man who points out how the strong man stumbles, or where the doer of deeds could have done them better. The credit belongs to the man who is actually in the arena, whose face is marred by dust and sweat and blood; who strives valiantly; who errs, who comes short again and again, because there is no effort without error and shortcoming; but who does actually strive to do the deeds; who knows great enthusiasms, the great devotions; who spends himself in a worthy cause; who at the best knows in the end the triumph of high achievement, and who at the worst, if he fails, at least fails while daring greatly, so that his place shall never be with those cold and timid souls who neither know victory nor defeat.

—Theodore Roosevelt

Appreciation for the Passionate Givers

Thank you for joining with us in the arena, for making dreams come true, and for being tremendous givers in so many ways!

We deeply appreciate our friends, who loved their team with unbelievable commitment and gave so much to impact their program.

You gave so much of yourselves to make an enormous difference in the lives of our players and your actions will benefit generations.

Bucky and Cynthia Allshouse

Steve and Shelby Butterfield

Martin and Monnie Calfee

Mike and Pat Case

Joe and Missy Cosgrove

Verde and Cathy Dickey

Jack and Debra Furst

Brad and Isabella Grow

Bill and Julie Kent

Ed and Karrin Robson

We are overwhelmed with gratitude for our relationship with you and the memories we share on and off the football field. We look forward to making more.

Remembering Butterfield
The Captain of the 7 C's

Steve Butterfield had a wonder about him. No one, no matter what they did, could deny the inviting presence of Steve Butterfield. Often called "Butter," Steve was one the biggest supporters of the Arizona State University's football program. Unfortunately, he lost his battle with heart issues, I think, because his heart was so huge. With heavy hearts, people have looked at the legacy of "Butter" and found his generous support and can-do attitude. **His legacy in and devotion to the art of athletics is surely one of the greatest seen in this generation.**

Summary of Todd's Career
from The Sun Devils' Website

Todd Graham made it clear he was a visionary. A throwback. A teacher who truly believes in the virtues of hard work, dedication and giving back.

He had a plan to infuse the program with a culture that was about winning in all facets of a student-athlete's life. Graham referred to it simply as, "The Sun Devil Way."

Graham, the 2013 Pac-12 Coach of the Year, concluded his sixth season at the helm of the Arizona State University football program. Under his leadership, Sun Devil football has reached levels of success not seen in more than 30 years.

2013 Pac-12 Coach of the Year

The Sun Devils won 46 games in six seasons at ASU – the most for a six-year span in Tempe since winning 46 from 1982–87. Graham is one of just three coaches (Frank Kush and Darryl Rogers) to win at least 30 games in their first four seasons at ASU. The 46 wins are third for any head coach in history (behind Kush and Bruce Snyder).

Individually, Sun Devils have accounted for over 50 Pac-12 All-Conference honors (51), numerous All-American awards—including a pair of consensus All-Americans in Will Sutton and 2016 Lou Groza Award winner Zane Gonzalez—and more than 30 student-athletes that were either selected in the NFL Draft or signed to free agent contracts.

He became the only ASU head coach to be bowl eligible in each of his first four seasons with the program and led ASU to bowl eligibility in five of six seasons—second-most at ASU behind Frank Kush's seven Bowl Games.

During his tenure at ASU, Graham was 10–12 against AP-ranked opponents. Those 10 wins are tied for the school record at ASU with Frank Kush and Bruce Snyder, despite coaching in fewer seasons than both of those coaches. His 10 wins more than doubled the Top-25 win total of Dennis Erickson (3) and Dirk Koetter (2) during their tenures. In the previous 14 seasons prior to Graham's arrival at ASU, the Sun Devils were a combined 5-40 in games against teams ranked in the AP poll.

Graham successfully instilled a culture of discipline during his tenure in the Valley of the Sun, guiding ASU to an average of just 37.4 penalty yards per game since the 2012 campaign. That mark was good for the fourth-lowest total in the country behind only Navy (27.3), Georgia Tech (36.7) and Army (37.1). The Sun Devils finished 19th or better in fewest penalty yards per game in five of six seasons under Todd Graham, and ranked no worse than 52nd during his time as a head coach in Tempe.

Since Graham arrived in Tempe, ASU has received 45 All-Pac-12 Conference recognitions, and 50 All-Conference academic honors, solidifying a culture of winning on and off the field. Sixty-five student-athletes earned Scholar Baller recognition for the 2016-17 academic year, and 431 Football Scholar-Athletes have been named Scholar Ballers in eight semesters under Todd Graham. 33 members on the roster have a cumulative GPA over 3.00.

Additionally, the team as a whole has posted over a 3.00 team GPA for the first time in program history as of summer school classes entering the 2017–18 academic year.

Graham became well-known on the national scene following a four-year stint at Tulsa (2007–2010) where he led the Golden Hurricane to a 36–17 mark, which included three bowl wins and three seasons of 10-plus wins. Tulsa was one of just 11 schools to post back-to-back 10-win seasons in 2007 and 2008.

The native of Mesquite, Texas, had seasons at Tulsa which included records of 10–4 (2007), 11-3 (2008) and 10–3 (2010) and in his final season the Golden Hurricane won games at Notre Dame and then topped No. 24

Posted back-to-back 10-win seasons

Hawaii 62–35 in its own bowl game. The Notre Dame win was dubbed the biggest upset of the 2010 college football season by ESPN's Kirk Herbstreit.

One distinguishing characteristic of Graham-coached teams has been their propensity for lighting up the scoreboard. On two occasions

Tulsa led the nation in total offense (2007 at 543.9 yards per game and 2008 at 569.9 yards per game) and ranked fifth in 2010. His 2010 Tulsa team also led the nation in interceptions (24) and was third in turnovers gained (36). His 2007 squad not only led the nation in total offense at 543.9 yards per game, it set 29 school records, 15 conference marks and four NCAA records. Tulsa routed Bowling Green 63-7 in the GMAC Bowl, the largest bowl margin of victory in NCAA history.

Graham's 2008 team again led the nation in total offense (569.9 yards per game) while ranking second in scoring (47.2 points per game), fifth in rushing (268 ypg), and ninth in passing (301.9 ypg). His team finished 11-3, capped by another large bowl win, a 45–13 victory over No. 22 Ball State in the GMAC Bowl.

Including ASU's 62–8 win over Navy in the 2012 Kraft Fight Hunger Bowl, Graham's offense has enabled three different teams (two at Tulsa) to score 60-plus points in a bowl game, making him the only coach to accomplish the feat multiple times.

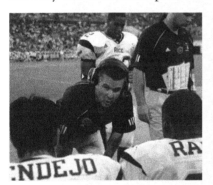

Graham led Rice to its first bowl game in 45 seasons.

Prior to taking the head job at Tulsa, Graham led Rice to its first bowl game in 45 seasons in 2006 and earned Conference USA Coach of the Year honors that same season.

Graham began his coaching career in 1988 as an assistant at Poteet High School/Middle School in Mesquite (1988–90) and then helped lead East Central University from a .500 program to NAIA national champions in his third year as he served as defensive coordinator from 1991–93. One year later he was at Carl Albert High School in Midwest City, Okla., and then spent time from 1995–2000 at Allen High School in Allen, Texas. While at Allen, north of Dallas, he also served as athletic director and led a program that had no district wins in the year prior to his arrival to five playoff berths in six seasons (1995–2000).

Graham was hired as the linebackers' coach at West Virginia in 2001, and one year later he was promoted to defensive co-coordinator as the Mountaineers went from 3–8 to 9–4, the top turnaround in the country in 2002.

Playoff game at Texas Stadium

In 2003 Steve Kragthorpe hired Graham as the defensive coordinator at Tulsa. For the second time in as many years, a Graham-led defense proved instrumental in helping a program post the nation's best turnaround as the Golden Hurricane went from 1–11 in 2002 to 8–5 in 2003. Graham's defenses would help lead Tulsa to a pair of bowl games before he moved on to take over the head job at Rice.

Graham was an all-state defensive back at North Mesquite High School and, after graduating in 1983, he played for East Central University in Ada, Okla., where he was a two-time NAIA All-American defensive back.

Born Dec. 5 1964, Graham earned his bachelor's and master's degrees in education from East Central University. He and his wife, Penni, have six children: Bo, Natalie, Hank, Haylee, Dakota, and Michael Todd Jr.

R. C. Slocum, One of Todd's mentors

Todd Graham Background

Overall Head Coaching Record: 95–60 (12th season)

Born: Dec. 5, 1964

Hometown: Mesquite, Texas

Alma Mater: East Central University (1987)

Family: Wife Penni and children Bo, Hank, Natalie, Haylee, Dakota, and Michael Todd Jr.

Year	School	Overall	Conference	Notes
2006	Rice	6-6	6-2 C-USA	Second in the West Division
2007	Tulsa	10-4	6-3 (C-USA)	First in West Division
2008	Tulsa	11-3	7-2 (C-USA)	Tied for first in West Division
2009	Tulsa	5-7	3-5 (C-USA)	Third in West Division
2010	Tulsa	10-3	6-2 (C-USA)	Tied for first in West Division
2011	Pittsburgh	6-6	4-3 (Big East)	
2012	Arizona St.	8-5	5-4 (Pac-12)	Tied for second in South Division
2013	Arizona St.	10-4	8-1 (Pac-12)	Pac-12 South Champions
2014	Arizona St.	10-3	6-3 (Pac-12)	Tied for second in South Division
2015	Arizona St.	6-7	4-5 (Pac-12)	
2016	Arizona St.	5-7	2-7 (Pac-12)	
2017	Arizona St.	7-5	6-3 (Pac-12)	Second place in South Division
	ASU Career	46-31 (6) 95-60 (12)	31-23 (6)	

Postseason Appearances under Todd Graham				
2005	Tulsa	Liberty Bowl	W, 31-24	Assistant Head Coach
2006	Rice	New Orleans Bowl	L, 41-17	Head Coach
2007	Tulsa	GMAC Bowl	W, 63-7	Head Coach
2008	Tulsa	GMAC Bowl	W, 45-13	Head Coach
2010	Tulsa	Hawai'i Bowl	W, 62-35	Head Coach
2012	ASU	Kraft Fight Hunger Bowl	W, 62-28	Head Coach
2013	ASU	National University Holiday Bowl	L, 37-23	Head Coach
2014	ASU	Hyundai Sun Bowl	W, 36-31	Head Coach
2015	ASU	Motel 6 Cactus Bowl	W, 42-43	Head Coach

Todd Graham College Coaching Experience

East Central University: 1991–93, defensive coordinator

West Virginia: 2001–02, co-defensive coordinator

Tulsa: 2003–05, assistant head coach and defensive coordinator

Rice: 2006, head coach

Tulsa: 2007–10, head coach

Pittsburgh: 2011, head coach

Arizona State: 2012–December 31, 2017, head coach

Other highlights from Graham's six seasons include:

- ASU was 30–10 at Sun Devil Stadium under Todd Graham, the second-highest number of wins for any Sun Devil coach.
- ASU was 31–23 in Pac-12 Conference games since 2012, the second-best total in the Pac-12 South behind USC (36–17).

Game days left me speechless.

- ASU was second in the nation in averaging 3.10 sacks per game since 2012. Additionally, ASU was first in the Pac-12 and second in the nation (Clemson) with an average of 7.7 TFL per game under Graham (since 2012).
- The Sun Devils forced 143 turnovers under Todd Graham, which was tied for the 17th-highest total in the country from 2012–17.
- ASU had 16 interception returns for touchdowns under Graham, compared to posting just four combined in the three previous seasons prior to 2012. The total was tied with Ohio State for first in the nation during that time.
- ASU added four fumble return touchdowns as well as 20 defensive touchdowns since the 2012 season, good for fourth in the country in that time span behind Ohio State (25), Alabama (22) and Boise State (22).
- ASU was ranked 9th in the nation with a .51 average turnover margin per game since Graham took over the helm, and 9th in the nation with a +38 total turnover margin since 2012.
- The Devils were second in the Pac-12 and tied for 10th in the nation with 91 total interceptions in that span.
- The Sun Devils rushed for over 2,000 yards five times in Todd Graham's six seasons at ASU (2,159 during the 2017 season) after doing so just one single time from 2000–2011 and only eight times total over 30 years from 1981–2011.
- ASU was ranked second in the Pac-12 and 15th in the nation at 35.9 points per game in the Graham era.[1]

Todd and Landon Finton leading the team onto the field.

---

[1] https://thesundevils.com/coaches.aspx?rc=673&path=football

Notes from Fans

The following are some of the Facebook posts on my page November 26, 2017.

Many more posts and letters and texts followed, but it is this day the messages meant so much. We were starting a new journey. The love in all the messages that day gave me incredible hope and courage. Thank you to all who have lifted us up over the decades through your love, kindness and generosity.

Robert Morris

Penni, I just want you to know we love you and Todd so much. I just wanted to mention what a good inspiration and role model he is for not only for the young men he coaches but, for all of us that know his story. Tell him thank you from so many fans.

David Reich

Penni, I'm a lifetime board member of the Sun Devil Club and I'm writing to tell you how sorry I am to see the news. ASU is blessed to have had Todd and your family leading our program and I know the ASU community will miss you both dearly. I wanted to personally thank you for all the love and passion you and Todd displayed for Arizona State during your time with our program and wish you great success in the next chapter of your lives.
Sincerely,

Brian Lee

Thank you, Graham family, for representing our university with the highest levels of class and character. We will root for Coach Graham and your family wherever you go. You leave ASU better than when you arrived. Your family created a team that we could be proud of again. Thank you for being great Sun Devils.

Terrance Ragains

You and coach had an incredible influence on the program at the time we most needed it. Thank you both for being amazing role models for the kids. The decision is questionable, and I'm very sad to see you go. Best of luck to you and I will always be a Coach Graham fan.

Paul Babb

Both you and Coach turned boys into men. You both preached character and discipline above all else. It's apparent how much ASU means to you. You will land something better and turn it into something better than you can imagine. You both mean a tremendous amount to my son and me. Love to you and Coach.

Alecia Strong

Thank you for all you and your husband did for ASU. Your love for my nephew and all of the athletes has impacted them more than you'll ever know. God's plans are definitely the best.

Ross Meyer

Thank you to you and your family. Today sucks. The way you and your family have treated ASU and its fans has been nothing but class. I am a Graham family fan and will be rooting for you all wherever you go next. In a world that doesn't have these characteristics as much anymore, you guys really stand out and practice what you preach. Thank you.

Eveyette Mendoza

Hey, Mrs. Graham, I just wanted to say I know God has amazing things in your future. I met your husband when I was in the Sun Devil marching band. Even from my first introduction Couch Graham has always showed me nothing but respect. I'm so proud of what he's done for my university and changing the culture of ASU. Good luck to the adventure that awaits you and thank you and your family for being a part of the sun devil nation.

Rande Grover

Give Coach my best. I appreciated all he did for the ASU program. You and Coach Graham are class acts. Go Devils!!

Robert Nathan

And that is what you gave to us. Heart, soul, character and a vision of what collegiate athletics should be. Thank you both.

Eddie Grant

Big time respect and admiration for both you and Coach. You are a fantastic first lady, and I am proud to call you a friend. (ASU Football 1989)

EPILOGUE

Suzanne Weis Dickey

You and Todd have the best attitude ever!! Shows who you really are! Everyone knows you put your heart and soul in this team and ASU and how you embraced PHOENIX! It's a very tough business, and you accomplished a lot in a short time! Lots of love. Go Devils.

Kyle Hall

Hey, from just a random ASU Alum and season ticket holder, we love both you and Coach Graham! I'm so sad to see you go, but thankful that you got to be here with us for 6 great years. I always have loved the way Coach Graham lived out his faith and brought character and integrity to our program. May God bless you both greatly wherever you end up next! I hope you will always consider yourselves Sun Devils wherever you go!

Brandan M. Spradling

Thank you for being a friend. You both did it all with much class and grace. I look forward to keeping up the friendship and following you on your next endeavors.

Travis Breedlove

Penni, you don't know me from any other fan out there. I want to say thank you to you, your family, and Coach Todd Graham: I'm a sad Sun Devil today, but I will always cherish this one event that happened in the first few months Coach was on the job. Six years ago, I took my son, who was three at the time, to the spring game. I wanted to meet Coach and get his signature in my Sun Devil History book. My boy was tired and grumpy, and it was hot. He was ready to go home. Todd looked at me and my son and shook both our hands as we welcomed him to ASU. Todd then did the kindest and most genuine thing anyone has ever done. It was so simple and little, but it sure brought a smile to my son and me. He took off his whistle and put it around my son's head. My boy's face lit up, and he wouldn't take off that whistle for days and kept talking about his coaches' whistle. A simple kind gesture will be ingrained in his head, and my heart thanks Coach Graham. Thank you again; I will always be a Graham family supporter.

David Hurley

Pure class as always, Penni! This is the first time I have ever cried upon hearing about the dismissal of a coach. It's obvious to anyone how much passion for the program and love for the players you and Coach have. I will root for the Graham family wherever your journey takes you. You will be missed and never forgotten for the impact you've had on the program. I want you to know this story: my wife is an elementary school teacher in a West Phoenix. She was named Arizona Teacher of the Year a few years ago. Her presentation included her take of Todd Graham's "Speaking Victory" philosophy to elevate her students in the classroom. What Todd has done has helped shape more than just the lives of the staff and students at ASU. God bless!

Warren Brannoch

I can't imagine how you feel. Heck, I've cried a few times since I heard the news. I've always been a Sun Devil fan since I was a little boy. Always dreamed of playing one day on Frank Kush field. When I finally got to college, I did play on Frank Kush field, but it was for the band :). Sometimes God has different plans for all of us. I for one am so humbled, and appreciative to have had the honor to meet Coach and you, and even though I've always been proud to be a Sun Devil, I'm prouder of the program than I've ever been. Watching Coach in his press conference the other day gave me peace that he is at peace. Best of wishes and prayers to you and your family, you'll be so missed! GO DEVILS!

Phil Alvarez

So proud of the accomplishments that occurred under CTG and blessed to have had Penni Leigh Graham as the Queen of ASU; they will forever be in our hearts!! Thank You!!!

Keola Loo

Aloha, Miss Penni and Coach Graham. Wanted to send my condolences to both of you and also to say thank you for allowing us to apart of the Sun Devil Family. We had a blast, and the memories will last a lifetime. Coach, thank you for allowing me to be a part of the coaching staff and opening up doors for me in this profession. Aloha and Mahalo from the Loo Ohana!!

Karen Husted

I am deeply sorry to hear this news. My husband and I have tremendous respect for everything you have done for our program, and we wish you the very best. You and Todd will be missed! Karen Husted SDMB

ACKNOWLEDGMENTS

*"I am a writer. If I seem cold, it's because
I am surrounded by drafts."*
—Unknown Author

When I started writing, I thought it would be a lonely process. It was the opposite. I deeply appreciate the informal committee who received text messages from me at all hours over these last months asking for their opinions.

Tony Jeary, my book coach, was invaluable; without his support, I would still be on chapter one. His team led me through a process that was so valuable in accelerating the writing process. Tony conveyed the spirit of a warrior with his insightful guidance and persistent mentoring!

Larry Carpenter, my publisher, with his lightning-fast responsiveness and limitless sources of information, made the process fluid, fun, and fabulous.

Lori Martinsek's amazing team at Adept Content Solutions for their incredible heroic work on my copyedit, stunning book cover, and intelligent interior designer captured my dreams and made *Tenacious* more attractive and interesting.

Content Editor Tiarra Tomkins for her insight and recommendations.

Our cover photographer, Stephanie Heymann, and the many other people who sent me photos and took photos for me over the years!

Craig Carpenter, website creator, made creating an author website quick and simple.

In addition to morale and intellectual and creative support, Natalie and Kaili Boos web and graphic design made my heart sing!

Tracey Tague with T2 Strategic Marketing Solutions for creating and supporting a Tenacious marketing plan.

Additional people helped shape the book with their words and editing, research and answering my text messages at three a.m: Nonie, Bo, Dakota, April, Wendy, Haley Margaret, Alexis, Janice, Sharon, Jay, Jonathan, and Linda.

My husband for helping and believing in me and living through this process, and my children for their encouraging words and support. I apologize that Door-Dash became your only source of meals for months. And for when I snapped or growled at you because I was focused on writing.

Without God's hands helping me, I could not have written *Tenacious*. In times of frustration and angst, He always blessed me with discernment and the courage to move forward.

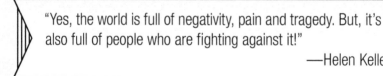

"Yes, the world is full of negativity, pain and tragedy. But, it's also full of people who are fighting against it!"

—Helen Keller

FOR THOSE WHO I WANTED TO ACKNOWLEDGE, INCLUDE, OR DEDICATE

I wish I could have included everyone I love and appreciate in one book. It would have been encyclopedic.

Only when it was necessary for story or quotes did I include names. Otherwise, I left people anonymous.

With storytelling, I had to make broad strokes over years.

I did not want to include a name without the advantage of a background story for readers.

I did not have room for, even some of our craziest, funniest stories.

Seriously, the blessing of a big life is the enormous number of people who you love, learn from, and appreciate.

I hope this book is a loved by many; I can write the ten books I cut during the process of the first.

I want to give a shoutout to my Facebook friends, whether or not we have met.

Over the years, you have been a limitless source support and wisdom.

With writing a first book, I asked hundreds of people for their help, opinions and input; so many people gave me a critical eye and encouraged me throughout the process. I deeply appreciate you.

To my family, friends, church families and leaders and everyone Todd and I have worked with over our lifetime.

You helped us grow and become champions of change!

Grateful for you *all*!

THECHAMPSOFCHANGE.COM

Go to

TheChampsofChange.com

to join become part of the

Tenacious Family and find new,

enlightening and entertaining

blog post, resources,

information, stories, and

activities to lead you on your

Tenacious Journey!

227

THE GRAHAM GAME PLAN

Professional and Personal
Development and Coaching

CHARACTER, SMART, DISCIPLINED, AND TOUGH

"Coach Todd Graham embodies the design-driven life.
His vision is clear and his passion is tangible. From a
room full of young athletes to a conference center full of
seasoned business executives, he elevates the belief and
ambition of anyone looking to grow and achieve."

*Chris Stuart is CEO of HSF Affiliates LLC and CEO
and president of Berkshire Hathaway Home Services.
Coach Graham recently spoke at Berkshire
Hathaway team event and received a
standing ovation.*

In today's world, the four characteristics critical to effective leadership—*Character*, *Smart*, *Discipline*, and *Tough*—are in short supply. Instead of simply demanding results, today's leaders need to coach those they lead on how to achieve their goals—how to bring out the best in those they lead.

Todd and Penni Graham know this better than anyone. Todd is a former D-1 NCAA head coach who has led young men to achieve more than they or the pundits ever thought possible. Penni is his rock, and a successful educator who has been at the cutting edge of education theory and practice.

Using their family and coaching motto of "Character, Smart, Disciplined, and Tough" and building upon decades of successful engagement, Todd and Penni will show any organization and the individuals who compose it how to reach their God-given highest potential.

Todd and Penni Graham apply the principles of this book to companies and organizations, showing leaders how to make their team members display the qualities of "Character, Smart, Discipline, and Tough" to exceed expectations, develop a culture of excellence, coach individuals to be their best, strengthen values, and be better leaders by learning the principles of successful coaching.

Key Objectives

Through on-site speaking, coaching, and consulting as well as online training, workshops, and seminars, Todd and Penni will help your team:

- **Embed "character" as a core trait in the lives of your team members.**
- **Show people that "smart" isn't a function of intelligence, but a way of making the right decision.**
- **Create an ability for individuals to exceed their expectations personally, professionally, and as members of a team.**
- **Increase organizational energy by boosting individuals' discipline to stay on task through every obstacle, uncertainly, or adversity.**
- **Teach self-management skills that make team members mentally, emotionally, physically, and spiritually tough to tackle challenges and secure the organization's future.**

Go to *TheChampsofChange.com* to request more information.

It is never too late to become whoever you want to be.

Let go of the monkeys!

Miracles and dreams await you!

CPSIA information can be obtained
at www.ICGtesting.com
Printed in the USA
BVHW061922190919
558939BV00001B/1/P